FOR PUTIN AND FOR SHARIA

A VOLUME IN THE NIU SERIES IN
Slavic, East European, and Eurasian Studies
Edited by Christine D. Worobec

For a list of books in the series, visit our website at cornellpress.cornell.edu.

FOR PUTIN AND FOR SHARIA

DAGESTANI MUSLIMS AND THE ISLAMIC STATE

Iwona Kaliszewska

Translated by Arthur Barys

NORTHERN ILLINOIS UNIVERSITY PRESS
AN IMPRINT OF CORNELL UNIVERSITY PRESS
Ithaca and London

Copyright © 2023 by Cornell University

All rights reserved. Except for brief quotations in a review, this book, or parts thereof, must not be reproduced in any form without permission in writing from the publisher. For information, address Cornell University Press, Sage House, 512 East State Street, Ithaca, New York 14850. Visit our website at cornellpress.cornell.edu.

First published 2023 by Cornell University Press

Library of Congress Cataloging-in-Publication Data

Names: Kaliszewska, Iwona, author | Barys, Arthur, translator
Title: For Putin and for Sharia : Dagestani Muslims and the Islamic State / Iwona Kaliszewska ; translated by Arthur Barys
Description: Ithaca [New York] : Northern Illinois University Press, an imprint of Cornell University Press, 2023. | Series: NIU series in Slavic, East European, and Eurasian studies | Includes bibliographical references and index.
Identifiers: LCCN 2022022630 (print) | LCCN 2022022631 (ebook) | ISBN 9781501767623 (hardcover) | ISBN 9781501767630 (paperback) | ISBN 9781501767654 (pdf) | ISBN 9781501767647 (epub)
Subjects: LCSH: Islam—Russia (Federation)—Dagestan. | Muslims—Russia (Federation)—Dagestan. | Islam and state—Russia (Federation)—Dagestan.
Classification: LCC BP65.R8 K35 2023 (print) | LCC BP65.R8 (ebook) | DDC 297.09475/2—dc23/eng/20220711
LC record available at https://lccn.loc.gov/2022022630
LC ebook record available at https://lccn.loc.gov/2022022631

Contents

Prologue: Pizza with Shakhidkas vii

Introduction 1

1. Political and Social Instability in Dagestan 20
2. Torture, Exorcisms, and Checkpoints: Experiencing the "Fight against Terrorism" 29
3. The Resurgent Importance of Islam in the Everyday Life of Dagestanis 53
4. Wahhabis, Tariqatists, and "New Muslims" 66
5. Sharia: Thinking beyond the (Secular) State? 84

Conclusion 129

Epilogue 134

Acknowledgments 137
Notes 139
References 145
Index 151

PROLOGUE

Pizza with *Shakhidkas*

The windows of the bedroom looked out onto the newly renovated boulevard leading to Lenin Komsomol Park in Makhachkala, the capital of Dagestan, the most unstable of Russia's North Caucasian republics. A young woman in her early twenties, dressed all in black, sat with her hands in her lap on the edge of an open sofa bed draped in a beige fleece blanket with a pink floral pattern. The cream-and-gold wallpaper behind the sofa looked as if it had been put up before perestroika.

"This is Aishat," said Murat,[1] who introduced her and then himself as the girl's guardian and brother in faith. He looked about thirty, thirty-five years old and identified as a Salafi, a follower of a puritanical form of Islam known as Salafism, or in the words of this community, a "true Muslim." Aishat welcomed me with a nod.

Aishat was born in a Lezgin village in the south of Dagestan. The Lezgins are the third largest ethnic group in the republic, which is home to fourteen officially recognized ethnicities and hundreds of other ethnolinguistic groups. She met Murat on the Russian social media site VKontakte. Inspired by his lifestyle and deep faith, she began to pray and soon put on the hijab. Her parents might have stomached their daughter's sudden whim if the clothing were at least colorful. However, the images conjured by the black hijab were unambiguous. Raised in Soviet times, Aishat's parents were religious in a way that was acceptable to their peers and elders in the community: they participated in *mawlids*, or celebrations of the Prophet Muhammad's birthday,[2] and attended mourning rites and other life-cycle events. They looked back on the USSR with a tinge of nostalgia and perceived the young people who were spreading knowledge about Islam in the region as a threat to their traditions and security.

"My family won't see me until I take off my hijab. They think I've been brainwashed or 'zombified,'" Aishat said. She gazed out the window and fell silent for a moment. "I ran away to the city. They are like a family to me now. Even closer than my own family." It was only then that I saw two young women, dressed in black, standing in a doorway. "This is Medina and Zeinab." Aishat pointed first

vii

to the woman in her early twenties with a round, childish face and then to the short brunette who, at around twenty-five, seemed the oldest of the two.

Aishat, Medina, and Zeinab shared a rented apartment in the center of Makhachkala. They all worked for Murat, whom they had met online. They came to the city from different corners of Dagestan. As children, each spoke a different language that was unintelligible to the others: Aishat's mother tongue was Lezgin, Medina spoke Lak, and Zeinab was fluent in Avar. In the city, however, they all spoke Russian, the lingua franca in Dagestan. The young women were reticent to talk about their roots, and they did so without the pride that often accompanies the stories Dagestanis tell about their home regions.

"That's not important," Medina explains. "What matters is that we're all Muslims." "We're all *istinniye* [true] Muslims," Zeinab adds.

The neighbors viewed them with suspicion. To Dagestanis brought up in traditional households, the thought of a group of girls in their twenties living alone, unsupervised by relatives, is unimaginable. Even married women, if they're still young, are often cared for (or rather, monitored) by a family member. The frequent visits by Murat and other "brothers in faith" only made matters worse. "There are only two options: either the girls are prostitutes, or they are future *shakhidkas* [female martyrs]," a friend of mine, considered "progressive" by the local intelligentsia, told me in no uncertain terms.

"Medina, Zeinab, get the things ready!" Murat ordered.

Medina and Zeinab took the blanket off the sofa bed, folded it in three lengthwise, and covered it with a linen sheet. Medina glanced at her watch and pulled three prayer mats out of the closet.

"Are we doing the *sunnah* prayers today?" she asked as she unrolled a small red rug depicting Mecca. The sunnah are an additional set of prayers performed by devout Muslims along with the five obligatory daily prayers.

"Sure, it's our duty," replied Zeinab. She continued straightening the sheet. Medina helped her tuck the edges under the folded blanket.

"I'm worried about that jeep over there," said Aishat, interrupting her prayers. "It wasn't there in the morning." Medina and Zeinab continued to pray. "Oh well, whatever happens will be the will of Allah," she added.

I approached the window to get a better look at the jeep. The dusty gray-green UAZ-496 was parked in front of the neighboring entrance; there was no one inside. When the prayer was over, Zeinab joined me. She did not continue the topic of the jeep.

"Nice view, isn't it?" she said, breaking the silence. "You know, we sometimes see Mukhu from this window. Mukhu is the president of Dagestan.[3] He likes to take walks in the park with his wife. His office is nearby," she said, a hint of excitement in her voice.

The conversation was interrupted by a knock at the door. "Just a moment," said Medina. Aishat suddenly rose from the sofa and began to tremble.

"Aishat! Aishat! Are you all right? Aishat?" shouted Zeinab. She and Medina helped the fainting girl down and carefully laid her on the sheet.

Murat burst through the door. A moment later, Abdul-Hamid entered. The rolled-up legs of his jeans were splashed with water, a sign that he had recently made his ablution and prayed. Abdul-Hamid slowly approached the girl on the floor, crouched, and pulled out his phone.

"They keep calling me to ask for a reading. I've got to remember to put it on silent." He smiled as he wiped the screen of his phone. Abdul-Hamid rearranged his light-blue shirt—semitransparent, revealing his torso—glanced at his watch, and opened a copy of the Koran.

"I need a blanket to cover her with," Abdul-Hamid said, turning to the girls. "She has to be covered from head to toe." He placed his hand on Aishat's head.

Abdul-Hamid had a part-time "job" reading the Koran over the ill. Reading—colloquially known as "expelling jinns"—is a craft he taught himself, inspired by the film *The Fifth Element*. He watched endless DVDs and YouTube videos, delving ever deeper into the art of exorcism. He began practicing it professionally after he tried his newfound knowledge on a sick cousin. The boy was cured, and Abdul-Hamid became convinced that it was his duty to help people in this manner.

Aishat experienced her first seizure at work, in the back room of the bakery run by Murat. She was taken to the municipal hospital, where the doctors were helpless. "Who would trust them anyway?" Zeinab concluded. In her view, all competent doctors had long left Dagestan. The only remaining ones were those who had bought their degrees or earned a living by taking bribes. Aishat's friends were concerned about her health; they wanted her to get better quickly so she could go back to work and resume her law studies. They placed great hopes in Abdul-Hamid.

Abdul-Hamid began to read: "Bismillah ir-Rahman ir-Rahim [In the name of God, the most gracious, the most merciful]." The woman's body began to convulse.

"Begone, enemy of Allah! Begone!" Abdul-Hamid fluently switched from Arabic *surahs* to guttural Russian. Aishat produced incomprehensible, at times animal-like, sounds. Abdul-Hamid stooped lower and lower over the girl, blowing into her covered face. Zeinab adjusted the blanket so that no part of Aishat's body would be visible. Medina recorded the whole operation on her phone. She gave me a sideways glance and smiled. Perhaps she had also noticed Abdul-Hamid's "Kalvin Klein" underwear band peeking over his belt.

"Begone, enemy of Allah!" Abdul-Hamid continued reading, now tapping Aishat's head with a *miswak* stick, a teeth-cleaning twig made from the wood of the arak tree.[4]

"Hold her down."

Murat, Zeinab, and Medina fell to the floor and together restrained Aishat, whose convulsions were becoming increasingly violent. Her long black hair spilled out from under the blanket.

The ceremony was interrupted by a sudden knock at the door. Zeinab quickly stood up. Images of masked soldiers raiding the apartment rushed through my head. Abdul-Hamid continued his recitation. Murat went out into the hallway. I recalled the stories I had heard about the hunt for "terrorists" and the raiding of apartments in Makhachkala. I knew Abdul-Hamid was on a "watch list," sometimes referred to as a "blacklist"—that is, an index of people classified as potential terrorists. The practice of reading the Koran raised red flags for security agents. They saw the ceremony as the first step on a path followed by future suicide bombers. Abdul-Hamid had already been paid a visit by the "Sixth Department," as the anti-terrorism unit is often referred to. There was no one home at the time but his wife and her girlfriends. The women managed to de-escalate the situation, and the raid was called off. Nevertheless, Abdul-Hamid expected the authorities to pay him another "house call," stage a provocation, or plant weapons or grenades in his home at any moment. Many of Abdul-Hamid's friends are dead. Weapons have even been "found" in the possession of those who did not know how to use them. The Sixth Department would take terrorism suspects away in unmarked cars, typically jeeps. Their bodies would later be planted at the scenes of special forces operations. Murat returned a moment later and made a calming gesture. I listened carefully throughout the rest of the reading, which went on for forty more minutes, "hearing" two more knocks on the door.

"That's enough for today. [The jinn] is still in there, but she's better now," said Abdul-Hamid, concluding the reading. He turned to Murat. "If that doesn't help, we'll need to do one or two more readings," he said, closing the door as he left the room.

Aishat slowly came to. "How was it? What happened?" she asked, adjusting her hijab. The terror had disappeared from her face and she suddenly became the smiling young woman I had seen before. She wanted to know if I had a husband and children, and whether I believed in God. She asked where Poland was and if any Muslims lived there. Zeinab peeked out the window. "The jeep's still parked outside. Maybe they were the ones who came by during the reading."

"I doubt it. I think it was the neighbors. They think we're some kind of terrorists because we wear black hijabs and rent an apartment together. Maybe they think we were training *shahids* today." Medina laughed.

"The pizza's almost here," Murat announced from the hallway. "I ordered one with chicken, one with vegetables, and one with olives. We don't want to burden the girls with the duties of traditional Dagestani hospitality. We'll do things the modern way. We'd just like you to make us tea later. OK?" he said, turning to Zeinab, who was already bustling about the kitchen and wiping teacups.

The pizza party in downtown Makhachkala turned into the telling of Abdul-Hamid's sad, and likely often-repeated, story of how easily one can end up being branded a terrorist by the authorities for being a Salafi. "They just need to have someone they can call a terrorist," Abdul-Hamid observed with disgust as he reached for the last slice of olive pizza.

FOR PUTIN AND FOR SHARIA

Introduction

It was not until 2013 that the attention of the media turned to Dagestan in the wake of the Tsarnaev brothers' bombing of the Boston Marathon. Tamerlan and Dzhokhar planted two homemade bombs near the finish line of the race, killing three people and injuring hundreds. The brothers had lived in Makhachkala before emigrating to the United States. In 2012, Tamerlan returned to Dagestan, where he was said to have met with and befriended local Muslims. What world would the twenty-five-year-old Tamerlan have encountered in 2012? What world were the five thousand Dagestanis who left for ISIS (among them policemen and civil servants) leaving behind? And what world were their widows and children coming back to?

Despite its recent stabilization, Dagestan remains the most unstable republic in the Russian Federation, plagued by violence and ubiquitous corruption. Calls for the creation of an Islamic state merge here with nostalgia for the days of Stalin's iron-fisted rule. Mecca prayer mats and calendars hang alongside pictures of Putin. People are not sure whom to fear more: terrorists or anti-terrorists? The Islamic State or the Russian state? How are we to make sense of these allegedly contradictory or even irrational notions through which the inhabitants of the North Caucasus attempt to imbue meaning into their reality?

The personal observations of two of my Dagestani interlocutors encapsulate these apparent contradictions.

2 INTRODUCTION

FIGURE 0.1. Troops heading to Dagestan, August 2012. Photo by Iwona Kaliszewska.

"I would like to be a patriot of my country, but they won't let me," Kurban, a fifty-year old former primary school teacher from the Dagestani lowlands, told me. As he spoke, he caressed his long red beard, which resembled that worn by the Prophet Muhammad. In June 2018, Kurban's two sons were dragged into a car in front of the house they were building. Kurban immediately went to the police station—not to report a kidnapping but to reclaim them.

"I had just married them off," he continued. "But I accept this situation with inner tranquility. The FSB [Federal Security Bureau] officers will not live forever. And they will answer to the Almighty," he added with more self-assurance and excused himself to perform his midday prayers.

Hizri, a Dagestani policeman in his thirties who shared a compartment with me on the train from Moscow to Makhachkala back in 2013, presented a different view. We were speaking over a glass of "real" Dagestani brandy that he had poured from a Fanta bottle, acquired from a friend who had swiped it from the distillery in Derbent. "Terrorists or FSB," he said, "there is no real difference between them." Hizri went on to recall stories where "the two" had co-operated to further destabilize the situation in the republic.

In order to understand what is actually disguised under "terrorism" and "counterterrorism" in the North Caucasus, I stayed away from official statements issued by security officials and politicians. I wanted to get a glimpse into the real everyday lives of such people as Kurban and Hizri, alleged terrorists and policemen, jinn exorcists, and fortune-tellers.

My attempts to describe the social reality of Dagestan gradually turned into examinations of the local experiences of the Russian state. How did the inhabitants of Dagestan experience state violence? What solutions did they see to the current situation in their republic? Should ostensibly radical expressions of support for sharia be interpreted in terms of resistance?

Attempts by Dagestani Muslims to regulate social life with rules such as fines for drinking, smoking, and not wearing the hijab have often been labeled as "imposing sharia" or as dangerous "attempts to create an Islamic state." Although such restrictions are often used as yet another way to control the lives of women, we should be wary of overemphasizing the strictness of sharia or its threat to secular order. A closer look at the Dagestani social reality reveals that what is often hidden behind the "imposition of sharia" is a world made up of people who, just like their secular friends, are concerned about the future of their corrupt and conflicted republic and who in their pursuit of a better social order turned, sometimes concurrently, to a number of models: social justice in the time of the Prophet Muhammad, Imam Shamil's nineteenth-century struggle for independence, the egalitarian and internationalist ideals of the USSR, and the strong states ruled by Stalin and Putin.

This book is an attempt to convey how Dagestani Muslims experienced both the "impositions of sharia" and the "fight against terrorism" between 2007 and 2019. The local dimensions of these phenomena provoke critical reflections on the essentialization and the Western centrism of these concepts and perspectives. By putting them in context, we can understand the very different ways in which they are experienced and invoked.

The social and political changes taking place in the Caucasus are often explained by examining the discourses of key political actors or content generated by people associated with the militant underground. At one end of the spectrum of discussion are debates attended by regional experts (analysts, politicians, and political scientists), held under such titles as "What Should Be Done about the North Caucasus?" and "Prospective Strategies for the North Caucasus"; at the opposite end are internet forums frequented by supporters of armed insurrection. Between the two is a broad range of alternative discourses, ideas, and visions. Similarly, the actions of the state, the violence of the security apparatus, and the violence of militants seeking to establish an Islamic state all bookend a vast space containing the everyday experience of the conflict. In contrast to the world of politicians and Kremlin advisers, this "alternative," "in between" world that demands change is one whose inhabitants directly experience chaos and cultural decay. These are the people who, just a few years ago, awaited change or expected it to come from the state, hoping that their lives would improve or that "Soviet-style order" would be reinstated. The experiences, narratives, and actions of these individuals form the space that I explore here.

This book is based on the experiences and narratives I gathered from conversations I had with Muslims in the Republic of Dagestan in the years 2007–2015 and on additional observations of life in Dagestan between 2004–2006 and 2016–2019, which I considered relevant to understanding the reality of the republic and the sociopolitical context of the issues discussed.

The years 2013–2014 marked a time when many Dagestani Muslims abandoned their hopes for a better or more just republic, opting instead to emigrate and build a future in the Islamic State. Among them were several of my interviewees. Hardly any of them returned. My description of the world of Dagestani Muslims, their problems, and their visions and hopes for the future offers a partial answer to the question of why they left and why some of them chose a highly uncertain future in the Islamic State over an intractable and unstable present in Dagestan.

My Field: Between the Secular and Religious Realms

Dagestan has a population of over three million people, with more than six hundred thousand living in the capital of Makhachkala, which was founded in 1844 as Port Petrovsk but was renamed in Soviet times after the communist hero Makhach Gadzhiyev. Among the main ethnic groups inhabiting the republic are Avars, Kumyks, Dargins, Tabasarans, Lezgins, Laks, Rutul, Mountain Jews, and Tats, as well as a dwindling Russian minority, which makes up 3 percent of the population.

The city center of Makhachkala, where my fieldwork began in 2004, resembles the ones found in many other Russian cities. It has a pedestrian boulevard running down the middle of Lenin Street (which now bears the name of the Dagestani poet Rasul Gamzatov) where *babushki*, or elderly women, sell sunflower seeds and nuts, and groups of young men loiter on stoops and benches. There is the obligatory Lenin Square, encircled by government buildings, the recently modernized Russia cinema, and a park commemorating the victims of the Great Patriotic War, with an "eternal flame" that went out in the 1990s and was only rekindled in 2005, when the park was renovated to mark the sixtieth anniversary of the end of World War II, or the Great Patriotic War.

INTRODUCTION 5

FIGURE 0.2. "Seeing how fiercely they defend their land and Russia, I'm beginning to like Dagestan and the Dagestanis more and more." V. V. Putin. Photo by Iwona Kaliszewska.

From 2004 to 2006, these places were my main points of reference in the city, centrally located landmarks linked by a network of perpendicular streets bearing the names typically found in the post-Soviet world: Kirov, Komsomolskaya, 26 Baku Commissars. Despite the mass renaming campaigns of the 1990s, the old nomenclature endured in the memory of the city's inhabitants and on the sheets of cardboard tucked behind the windshields of *marshrutkas*, or minibuses, announcing their destinations. Only the famous Bolshevik Mikhail Kalinin gave up his street to Imam Shamil, the religious and political leader of the Caucasian Muslims in their struggle for liberation from imperial Russia in the nineteenth century.

In the same meshwork of streets, mosques were an important presence: large and small, old ones with plastered walls and newer mosques built from Dagestani sandstone dotted with shells, fitted with white UPVC windows, and surrounded by soaring fences. Most of my interlocutors—at the time, local intellectuals—had never been to a mosque in their lives, much less attended regular prayers. Between 2004 and 2006, despite the prominent religious features and symbols visible in the public space, I saw the city as a "secular Makhachkala." Islam played no role in the lives of urban intellectual circles: neither the ones fascinated with Europe and ideas of liberal democracy nor the ones whose members recalled the Soviet era with a sense of nostalgia.

"Religious Makhachkala," in which I immersed myself in 2007, occupied the same familiar spaces. Yet, these were defined by a different set of landmarks: mosques, madrassas, halal grocery stores and restaurants, and shops with Islamic books, clothing, and cosmetics. Some of these locations were not immediately visible to passers-by. To find out where *hijama* (medicinal bloodletting) was practiced, who performed exorcisms or treated patients using herbal remedies, and which imams offered matchmaking services or encouraged men to take more than one wife, I had to inquire among "those in the know." Government offices, city squares, and public buildings were of secondary relevance here. They were neither "pilgrimage" destinations nor places of employment: the majority of my more devout interviewees eschewed government jobs, preferring to run their own businesses: stores, car washes, restaurants, and bakeries. My new interlocutors and friends—the newly forming religious elite and their followers in the middle and lower classes—would recognize the landmarks from the secular realm but preferred to meet at the Djuma or Tsumada mosque after midday prayers, or have a lunch at Maydat, a well-known halal restaurant.

In the latter years of the 2000s, religious Makhachkala began to increasingly encroach on the public space of the city. Signs were put up urging locals to place their faith in Allah and to pursue greater jihad or personal improvement. Billboards displaying images of scantily clad women were defaced and the word *haram* (forbidden) scrawled on them. Marshrutka drivers posted stickers reading "Free fare for girls in hijab." A growing number of women wore the hijab; new Islamic stores opened, including shops that catered exclusively to women and were explicitly off-limits to men.

"Secular Makhachkala" shrunk with every passing year. Some people emigrated; some, in particular the younger ones, immersed themselves in "religious Makhachkala," limiting ties with their former colleagues. Others stayed more or less loyal to their ideals. Former opponents—"democrats" and those who kept framed pictures of Stalin on their living-room walls—sat together in undercover clubs that still served liquor and jointly observed, with growing terror, the recent Islamization of the city and the mass migration from the mountains. They might have disagreed about the past, but they unanimously agreed on the present: "This isn't our Makhachkala anymore."

As much as I immersed myself in the rapidly expanding "religious Makhachkala," I never fully abandoned the secular one, often wavering between the two: attending get-togethers in the undercover clubs on one day and sitting in on jinn exorcisms the next.

This division between "religious" and "secular" Makhachkala and Dagestan is intended to serve as a metaphorical illustration of the shift in my per-

FIGURE 0.3. Veiled and unveiled students coming home from high school. Photo by Iwona Kaliszewska.

ception of people and places as well as the changes that occurred over several years. As my knowledge about the city deepened and expanded and as I grew more comfortable with this new space, what had once been hidden to me gradually became more interesting and comprehensible.

Although I initially focused my fieldwork on the city center of Makhachkala, the locations changed as my research progressed. I followed my interlocutors to their *jamaats*, or communities, and gradually drifted into the countryside, particularly to the Tsumadinsky District bordering Georgia and Chechnya. My actions and the form of my involvement were shaped by the numerous connections with which I had become entangled and were often beyond my control.

Sipping Coffee to the Sound of Gunfire: Conducting Fieldwork in Unstable Locations

Back in 2004, the media coverage of bombings, counterterrorism operations, kidnappings, and murders taking place in Dagestan struck me as overblown. The lack of vacationers in the deserted seaside resorts did seem odd, and the fortress at Derbent—a popular tourist destination in Soviet times—was strangely empty, but life went on as usual on the streets of Dagestani cities. My positive view of the republic was nevertheless marred by minor everyday issues, such as my hosts' excessive insistence that I come home before dark and avoid traveling alone, or the weapon (a Kalashnikov rifle) in the trunk of one of the cars I rode in; the driver, a man in his fifties, refused to comment on it, insisting that it was "a hunting rifle used for shooting bears." The sound of gunfire that could be heard from time to time made me doubt my local friend's assertions that the shots came from "cap guns" and that the weapons we saw were "probably air guns or mock guns." But minor flaws such as these did little to spoil the favorable image I had of Dagestan after the initial fieldwork for my master's thesis, which I had conducted there in the summer of 2004. I was there, after all, to explore ethnic issues, not war.

In late April 2005, rumors began to spread in Makhachkala that guerrilla fighters might attack the city. My host's sisters recommended that he stop writing about sensitive subjects and consider having his windows fitted with bars and a security door installed. One night that April, when I was staying in his apartment, an explosion rocked the city. I wanted to go see what had happened, but another closer blast dampened my curiosity. I was frightened, yet the violence continued to feel distant, intangible, and in a sense, nonexistent. Dagestanis themselves reinforced these feelings. "That war's far away," I'd hear from one interviewee, a man in his forties. "There's no war here; everything's calm and quiet. It's just the media making things up." "It's not like we're in Chechnya," his slightly older colleague added, trying to convince me to join him on his trip to the mountains at the beginning of May 2005. And yet, none of my acquaintances left town for the traditional May Day cookout, or *mayovka*. The "annual" mayovka, I later learned, had not been celebrated for several years.

When I returned to the republic in 2007 with my husband and seven-month-old daughter, we instantly became a fleeting local "attraction," "actual foreigners" who had driven all the way from Poland to Dagestan in a Lada Niva with Polish license plates. We gave interviews to eager Dagestani television stations and newspapers. They asked whether we had any apprehensions about driving to Dagestan and why we were not deterred by the reports of guerrillas and explosions that were a regular feature on Russian news broadcasts but, as we could see, had "nothing to do" with the local reality. "Knowing what not to know becomes not only an art of survival but the basis of social reality," Michael Taussig (2005, 12) writes. The tendency to shut oneself off from knowledge of a certain type as well as narrate self-delusional visions of reality were widespread survival strategies both among Colombian villagers during the cleansing as well as among my interlocutors. It was a kind of defensive strategy that allowed my Dagestani acquaintances and myself to perceive our own reality in terms of "normalcy."

Only after six months of regular fieldwork in Dagestan—once I had accrued sufficient experience and listened to enough personal stories—did my body begin to respond instinctively to dangerous situations. I found myself waking up more often in the night, taking ordinary sounds for possible gunshots. In Makhachkala, I stayed in the apartment of a divorced friend, provoking scornful stares and snide comments from his neighbors, yet I preferred these living arrangements to the prospect of living alone in a rented flat. On the few occasions that my host went away for a few days, I would go to great lengths to avoid spending the night alone in his empty apartment, often abusing the hospitality of my other friends. The experience of the next few years stripped away any illusions I had harbored about Dagestan as a peaceful republic. The summer holiday atmosphere was marred by the increasingly conspicuous weapons and OMON (Special Police Force) units deployed to the streets of Makhachkala. Weapons and police had been a regular feature of daily life throughout my research in Dagestan, but it was only after having listened to the personal stories and experiences shared by my interviewees that I began to perceive these elements of the security apparatus as instruments of violence, deadly tools that could be deployed at any moment. Familiar locations in Makhachkala acquired a different character. What was once a kiosk near my friend's apartment building became a shop that I dared not enter to buy a box of chocolates, so intimidated was I by the man in a black balaclava standing at the door. Nor did I fail to notice that the jazz club I used to visit had been sealed off from public view, and a "security guard" armed with a rifle had been posted in front, accompanied by a couple of heavyset men, each with a pistol tucked into their pockets. When I passed a damaged building, I immediately knew whether it was the result a "special operation" or some other event. I no longer saw broken windows as signs of children playing soccer in the streets. Rather, they were evidence of a passing shock wave triggered by a powerful explosion. I experienced a sense of anxiety as I walked or drove past a police station or even a parked police jeep. Marshrutka drivers gave these spots a wide berth and were careful not to stop nearby.

I initially perceived interrogations at the police stations or FSB as unpleasant but hardly rare in Russia: encounters that required you to stay calm and pretend to be a crazy tourist, and sooner or later you would be released. I tried to reframe them in a positive light, seeing them as opportunities to enrich my knowledge about the workings of the state. Eventually, however, I started to fear them as I imagined that the many conducting my interrogation could potentially be responsible for tortures and kidnappings. But aside from moments like these, my life in the republic went on as before, and I continued to meet with friends over tea or coffee and visit cafés and restaurants. Like other people living in Dagestan, I began to inhabit two worlds: one safe, the other gripped by violence. This state produced completely different, often conflicting, experiences and reactions. When I heard the explosion of a bomb, I would sometimes want to run to the blast site to see what had happened, while at other times I would panic at the sound of what turned out to be a cap gun. I lived in both dimensions at once, halfway between the ordinary and the extraordinary. Each provided independent points and frames of reference, spanning "controlled hysteria and tacit acquiescence" (Green 1999, 59). People are often aware that their lives straddle this boundary; the two territories interchange, each realm appearing exotic when viewed from the perspective of the other (Taussig 2005).

Student, Assistant, Mother, Correspondent

My fieldwork spanned fifteen years, and in this time, my personal status underwent a variety of transformations. I went from being a university student, to a mother with a child, to an expert. I went from being a girl who required aid and protection (a duty performed by the Aliverdiev family) to a person with whom one could discuss the problems facing the republic, who could report on Dagestan's situation in the Western press, and who could help locals secure a visa or leave the country. This shift in status was prompted not only by the knowledge and experience I was acquiring but also that I was learning to behave as women were expected to. It was also a result of my expanding network of acquaintances and the people who accompanied me on a given trip: my husband and child, a female or male colleague, or no one at all. As I ventured into the field, I gradually internalized a number of cultural proscriptions that apply to Dagestani women; I avoided shaking hands with men or sitting in the front seat of a marshrutka, instead choosing a seat next to other women whenever possible. I did not object when a male acquaintance paid for my meal or bus ticket. I also learned not to ask men for directions to the bathroom. If there were no women around, it was acceptable to ask a man where I could wash my hands. I understood that when visiting someone's home, if my hosts offered to let me wash my hands, they were in fact telling me I could use their bathroom. I made sure to wear a headscarf and a long skirt whenever I visited "religious Makhachkala" or the countryside. Whenever a man or older woman entered the room, I would stand or merely signal my intent to do so by rising slightly. These habits became so ingrained in my own gestures and reflexes that they persisted even after I returned to Poland. I gradually learned to ignore unknown men who attempted to strike up a conversation in the streets of Makhachkala or Derbent—men who reflexively assumed (if they realized that I was a foreigner) that I might be willing to "go for a shashlik picnic," "go out to a restaurant," or "have some tea together." There were many situations in which I had to resort to lying, "proving" my Dagestaniness (or pretending to have a telephone conversation) in order to embed myself within the local system and imply that the person had better watch what he does and says, or else he would have a local authority figure or "my brother" (whom I called Magomed) to deal with. Excuses such as "I am married" were largely useless and merely elicited incredulous laughter: "What kind of husband would let his woman go on such a long trip alone?"

Traveling in the company of a man was simpler, as it allowed me to avoid unwanted male attention, but it also immediately cast me as either a wife and mother (when I was with my husband and child) or as an "assistant" (when I was conducting fieldwork with a male colleague). In the former case, I would automatically be assigned to join the local women, who were eager to entertain my baby or pass her off to their older children so that we could have a conversation (see figure 0.5). They would ask why I had chosen to name my daughter Lena—a Russian name, in their view—and offered advice on how to treat a rash or shield an infant from evil spells. These women treated me like a young, inexperienced, and somewhat irresponsible mother who needed plenty of guidance, which I gladly accepted, as it gave me a chance to observe motherhood in its local context. The notion that I might be conducting fieldwork that occasionally touched on political topics was regarded with mild incredulity and even sarcasm at times. Within a single year I went from being a university student to being a mother with child, and that was my fundamental identity—one that posed an obstacle to my fieldwork but also enriched my experience as a researcher.

Conducting fieldwork with a male colleague, by contrast, enabled me to reenter the world of men. I would once again become a researcher—or more accurately, a research assistant. No matter which one of us asked a question, the response would be directed at my colleague. I initially found such situations irritating, but I eventually learned to take advantage of my "subordinate" status. If I found the conversation boring, I could slip away to join the women in the kitchen, an inappropriate move were I the only guest or if I were traveling with another woman.

As I made repeated solo trips, my circle of acquaintances broadened significantly, eventually encompassing people who were considered influential. I was promoted to the position of an expert who, despite initial doubts, understood

INTRODUCTION

FIGURE 0.4. Doing fieldwork with my baby daughter. Photo by Sebastian Kaliszewski.

the situation facing the republic and was in a position to report on it in the media. However I introduced myself to my interviewees, they inevitably perceived me as a journalist rather than an anthropologist. On more than one occasion, my host took advantage of my perceived status as a foreign correspondent to set up interviews for me with politicians and influential journalists—people with whom he had "business to take care of" and who would otherwise be reluctant to schedule a meeting with him.

FIGURE 0.5. Doing fieldwork with my baby daughter. Photo by Iwona Kaliszewska.

FIGURE 0.6. Preparing food for the *mawlid*, or collective prayer, Kayakent Region. Photo by Iwona Kaliszewska.

Due to the nature of my research, the majority of the subjects I initially interviewed were men. They were more forthcoming than women about their ideas for the future of Dagestan and were more eager to discuss the advantages of Islam and sharia and to talk about the role religion played in their lives. Even though I spent a comparable amount of time with women, whenever I asked them about religion or the republic, they would defer to the men, arguing that males were "more knowledgeable" about such subjects. The information I collected through interviews and conversations thus reflected a more masculine perspective. Women, I assumed in the early stages of my research, were nearly absent from men's debates about the state and society, appearing only occasionally to offer quiet commentary or to deconstruct male assertions. One acquaintance, in her thirties, bored by her husband's monologue, perked up at his mention of the equal rights men and women enjoyed in Islam. "Great. How about you do the dishes?" she muttered, laughing. Another woman, in her fifties, interrupted her son as he extolled the virtues of polygamy, and announced, "If you take a second wife, I'll kill you or kick you out of my house, and she [the first wife] will stay with us. You'll be gone before you know it!" Others would limit their commentary to gestures, smiles, or silence. Eventually, therefore, though I gathered more elaborate narratives from men, women's opinions on shariatization and their experiences of the state violence are also broadly present, albeit more often in the form of short comments, utterances, or silence.

What Remains Unwritten: Ethical Issues in Fieldwork

As I was researching my politically charged subject, at times touching on issues to which the label of terrorism is applied, I unwittingly stepped into a minefield of moral dilemmas. I encountered them in everyday conversations, while traveling, when concealing my own identity, and no less importantly, when writing and speaking about my own experiences. What could I write, and what should I leave unmentioned so as not to put anyone in danger? Was I justified in impersonating others through my choice of clothing and disguising the fact that I was a foreigner? Or was it rather a cultural appropriation? Could I write about these experiences, and if so, how?

The people to whom I talked were not always aware that I was a foreigner, much less an anthropologist. There were many instances in which it was safer for everyone involved if I hid my identity by disguising myself with the appropriate outfit. There is always a moral dimension to the knowledge that emerges from an encounter: we create an ethnographic self that is changed by the other, and vice versa. It is at the intersection of the self and the other that knowledge appears.[1] But what do we do with information that, as we later determine, has been gathered unethically or inappropriately? Regrettably, there were many instances of this sort throughout my fieldwork, and they were typically a result of my fears and the precautionary measures I took.

Methods such as impersonation and the use of disguises raise moral dilemmas, even when we are guided by security concerns and our respect for local custom. The way in which people spoke to me differed depending on whether they thought of me as a foreigner, someone who lived in Dagestan, or a Russian woman. When I was perceived as the second of the three, it was assumed that I would understand certain out-of-context statements and that there were matters that did not require any elucidation. In the third case, it was assumed that I had family in the republic: "What else would a Russian woman be doing in Dagestan?" I found it intriguing to have access to knowledge beyond what is typically revealed through conversations and actions associated with "pure" fieldwork. I grew to enjoy my new incarnation. I felt a sense of accomplishment as a field researcher and a Russian speaker. I was attracting much less attention from the police and the FSB. I traveled by marshrutka, and I would hang out in Islamic shops, dressed in the kinds of clothes typically worn by Dagestani Muslim women: a long, black skirt, a headscarf, and a tight top or dark sweatshirt. The clerks knew that I was from Poland, and I did not hide the fact from the customers, but my country of origin was not necessarily the first piece of information I shared with them. As I browsed through the cosmetics or the sermons on compact disc, people would sometimes approach me to recommend particular preachers or encourage me to try hijama (a practice I observed several times).

When these conversations went beyond a cursory exchange, I would usually tell my interlocutor that I was not a Muslim and that I came from Poland. But the opportunity to do so did not always arise, and sometimes I was held back by fear and distrust. Out of concern for my own safety and that of others, I preferred to remain anonymous, especially if an individual did not strike me as trustworthy. Furthermore, during the course of my research, I realized that many people would spend significant amounts of time with me not just because they were compelled to do so by the Dagestani tradition of hospitality but also because I was perceived as a potential convert to Islam. On the one hand, I made a point of describing the purpose of my research in honest terms, openly stating that my interests were purely academic. On the other hand, I took advantage of these circumstances in a more or less deliberate fashion.

The knowledge I gained was conditioned on a relationship of trust, which meant that no matter what I learned, I could not allow any harm to come to my interviewees as a result of what I wrote or said. The topics we discussed included violence and politics. In a town the size of Makhachkala, these accounts could easily be traced to specific individuals. I would use obfuscation techniques such as hiding names, not asking for identifying information "on tape," and refraining from recording certain conversations. But these methods were not always sufficient, particularly in sparsely populated areas. At the same time, by obscuring certain details and interfering too heavy-handedly in my depictions of a given place, I risked producing warped descriptions.

Political and social instability, the shariatization of Dagestan, and possible visions of the republic's future are all seen as controversial topics, ones that provoke interest and enjoy popularity not just in academic circles but also among journalists and people associated with think tanks and analytical institutions. Even though I hoped to engage in such discussions, I was also becoming increasingly wary that such research, even when conducted with full confidentiality, could be used against my informants or Dagestani Muslims in general. The ongoing debate in the United States and Western Europe over the use of anthropology and anthropologists by government institutions struck me as important, yet these problems did not seem relevant to my own fieldwork. I condemned the participation of anthropologists in the "war on terror" and the wars in Iraq and Afghanistan. Meanwhile, many people whom I encountered in the field believed that I was acting on behalf of the West. I was persistently questioned about my motives. "Who told you to study this? Why are you so interested in politics? Who are you researching this for?"; "I don't believe that you're researching this 'just because.' Someone must be paying you for it." My replies were met with suspicion. In the eyes of some interviewees, at least in the early phases of our relationships, I was a spy, someone on the payroll of the U.S. government, a British nongovernmental organization, or the Polish government, an alleged supporter of Chechen separatism. The motivations ascribed to me would vary, aligning to some degree with whatever explanation for the unrest in the Caucasus was currently viral in the media, but it always involved an external force of some sort.

The years 2009 and 2010 marked a turning point in my research. The problems facing the region were increasingly present in the public debate, and people had begun to openly discuss the issue of corruption and to voice their dissatisfaction with the "system" that had pervaded the Russian Federation.[2] The accusations of espionage were gradually becoming less frequent: I was now just a visitor from abroad, a correspondent, someone whom people could talk to about "this whole mess" and who might write about it back home to "let the world know what's going on here, what kind of injustice we have to live with."

In April 2010, as we[3] were recording video footage in downtown Makhachkala, we were approached by a middle-aged man who appeared ready to tell us that we were "not allowed to film here" and who, we suspected, would be upset that we were not filming the city's most attractive sights. Instead, he introduced himself, welcomed us to the city, asked where we were from, and openly said, "I'm glad you're filming this. If you want, I can tell you all about this, about all of the filth, all the corruption, all about how we live."

Information that I had previously regarded as confidential was being published online, often in the local press as well, particularly in the newspaper *Chernovik*. What was once a topic that I had trouble discussing in the field and later struggled to write about had become the subject of everyday conversations. Although I continued to practice the utmost discretion in my research, more and more people were eager to share their experiences with me and tell me their life stories. I had gone from being an anthropologist who dealt with uncomfortable topics to being a person who would gladly listen to those who longed to be heard, and this reinforced my faith in the purpose of my research and the risk I was taking. I took it on myself to describe the experiences of people affected by state violence, to relate the human dimension of the suffering caused in the name of the fight against terrorism. My goal was to illuminate this segment of reality not just for anthropologists but also for scholars in other fields—anyone who had turned a blind eye to the violence carried out by the state in its war on terror. As Nancy Scheper-Hughes (1995) argues, the anthropologist must engage with urgent issues and take the side of the disprivileged and victims of violence. This approach entails a certain political responsibility: it is a form of social advocacy in which the anthropologist becomes a witness rather than merely a dispassionate observer, explaining the problem to her readers, drawing their attention to instances of suffering or struggle, particularly when they involved the disprivileged. Research should stir public debate, influence public opinion, and even produce change. "Anthropology," Scheper-Hughes (1995) writes, "if it is to be worth anything at all, must be ethically grounded." Nevertheless, I began to perceive a potential threat in the approach proposed by Scheper-Hughes: although I had no doubt that the black-and-white approach of the war on terror had to be deconstructed somehow, I was wary about expressly supporting either side. Policemen and FSB agents also numbered among the victims of the conflict, regardless of whether they supported the "fight against terrorism." Meanwhile, though I had no doubt that it was my duty to conceal all the personal information of individuals who faced the threat of violence from the security apparatus, I did not always apply these standards to state officials. I did not obscure their names when mentioning them in writing, nor did I consider whether I had the right to use information I had gathered from conversations with these individuals, particularly when the purpose of these encounters was to question me. Only after the murder of Ahmed—an FSB agent in the Tsumadinsky District who spent time showing my colleague and me around the center of Agvali, the regional capital, and who, despite being a representative of the state himself, was candidly sharing his doubts about the counterterrorism measures deployed in the republic—did I become more sensitive to the security of those whose position of power, in my view, enabled them to fend for themselves. As I ventured deeper into the field, the reality of the conflict became increasingly blurred and ambiguous. Individuals suspected of "terrorist activity" were not the only victims of the conflict: they also included regular policemen and other state officials like Ahmed. They were killed for being representatives of the state, people associated with persecution and violence, regardless of their own involvement in such activities.

The complex power relations and escalating violence on both sides of the conflict meant that I was unable and unwilling to advocate for either side. Instead, I limited my involvement to prompting discussions and debates and to speaking out against violence, no matter the perpetrator or the justification offered by my interviewees. I realized how incomplete my own knowledge was,[4] and I thus strove simply to behave empathetically, to listen, see, and observe, and to share the space, the life, and the process in which knowledge is produced, even when I was completely at odds with my interlocutors. I did not hide my disapproval at hearing about the social benefits of murdering fortune-tellers, prostitutes, and policemen or that the only solution to the conflict was to "get rid of Wahhabis." I objected but did not ridicule their views in an attempt to learn as much as I could about the experiences of the person I was interviewing. Unable to help the people I encountered or to resolve their problems, I tried to make the best of my ability to listen carefully and to observe with empathy and compassion. This approach is occasionally referred to as compassionate fieldwork. "Not to look, not to touch, not to record can be the hostile act" (Scheper-Hughes 1995, 418), while to listen with empathy, to accompany another, and to share in their experience can be an act of solidarity and recognition.

"We all want simple truths. We want mysteries that give way to our probings. We want situations that yield to analysis. We want tried-and-true concepts to mean what they always have and the assurance that design and method can ultimately win out over randomness and entropy. And maybe more than anything, we want stories that have clear morals, heroes, and villains who are what they appear to be, and endings that finally end," David Edwards (2012, 356–67) writes.

But "just as anthropologists provide a space in their texts for analysis and interpretation, so should they leave room for strangeness and uncertainty."

Conducting several years of fieldwork in a time of turbulent political transformation was a frustrating experience: the political situation was undergoing serious changes, and individuals would express vastly different views as time went by. Although my observations and conclusions pertain to a specific period, it was precisely then that a fundamental shift took place: forced underground, Salafis (or those to whom that label had been affixed) were becoming increasingly numerous, and more and more people were openly criticizing the "system." The younger generation became the driving force behind the re-Islamization of the republic as well as the main subject of broader desecularization processes.

As I described my own experiences, I made an effort to constantly reflect on and contextualize them within the ongoing transformation, which I discuss in greater detail in the following chapter.

CHAPTER 1

Political and Social Instability in Dagestan

The North Caucasian Federal District remains a place in which violence, despite the recent stabilization, is a fixture of everyday life, where corruption is rampant and whose inhabitants try to pursue justice on their own. A growing number of Dagestanis, whether or not they support sharia, no longer engage with the state or do so for purely opportunistic reasons. Small business owners prefer to pay *zakat*[1] (alms) rather than taxes, claiming that they at least know where the money is going (Kaliszewska 2020); children are sent to private Islamic nurseries and kindergartens that serve halal food and teach the basics of religion. When a road or school is needed in a village, the region's wealthiest sons are called on to assist the project. A growing number of Dagestanis distance themselves from state practices, condemning them as morally reprehensible and incompatible with the values by which they strive to live.

The state lives on in memories of the USSR, in state symbols such as Putin and his portraits, statues of Lenin, and so forth (see figure 1.1), and in the persons of high-ranking state officials. The state may be valued positively and reified in some contexts while in others be perceived as a source of the unwarranted violence that affects many aspects of everyday life. The result is a widening gap between the North Caucasus and the rest of the Russian Federation, with the former subject to different social norms and only formally remaining within the jurisdiction of Russian law.

POLITICAL AND SOCIAL INSTABILITY IN DAGESTAN

FIGURE 1.1.   "Avenue of Heroes," the monument to the Great Patriotic War in Derbent. Photo by Iwona Kaliszewska.

The conflict between militants and the security forces, internal strife within state structures, pervasive corruption, and later, departures to join ISIS were the key elements of the political and social unrest in Dagestan. The most visible was obviously the armed conflict between the security forces and militants fighting under the banner of Islam. The militants' goal at the time was to establish an Islamic state that would encompass the republics of the North Caucasus, offering it as an alternative to the current system. Between 2009 and 2011, bombings and fighting between armed militants and state security forces occurred on a nearly daily basis, and political assassinations were also frequent. The targets of these attacks were public figures, businessmen, and people believed to be militants. In this period, Dagestan was undergoing what is now being described as a conflict or civil war. Special operations aimed at capturing "terrorists" were carried out almost daily. In 2011 itself, authorities conducted three hundred operations of this type; the fighting resulted in 824 casualties, including 413 deaths.[2] Bearing in mind the size of the republic and the number of inhabitants (nearly three million), these numbers are significant. Among the actors who stood to benefit from the conflict were the security forces (whose special operations require substantial funding), criminal organizations involved in drug trafficking and money laundering (conducted through shell companies and virtual banks), and individuals running protection schemes. Between 2013 and 2014, the open conflict between militants and security forces gradually waned, and explosions and special operations became less frequent. The militant underground was outnumbered in the run-up to the Sochi Olympics (Orttung and Zhemukhov 2017), and alleged or real militants were killed or arrested. Many Dagestanis left for ISIS. The reasons behind their departure varied: from feeling permanently threatened by local security forces, through rebellion against family members, to being lured by recruiters; the Federal Security Service of the Russian Federation (FSB) and local police did not hinder these departures. I came across cases in which families reported their loved ones to the police or FSB on the suspicion that they were about to leave to join ISIS. The security forces acted very reluctantly, if at all. Barely anybody who left returned to the North Caucasus. Those who survived stayed in Syria and Iraq or fled to Ukraine. The few who ventured home live fearfully under new identities; some have been imprisoned or placed under surveillance. Widows of ISIS fighters were, for the most part, left in peace, as they were believed to have no involvement in their husbands' actions, though this was not necessarily the case. Although the open conflict in the North Caucasus has lost its strength, as of 2020, the hidden conflict continues to permeate the everyday life of Dagestanis. Explosions, shootings, and special operations are no longer a permanent fixture of the local landscape, but kidnappings, murders of faith leaders, social activists, and journalists as well as murders tied to power struggles and the settling of personal or clan scores[3] continue to plague the republic.

The criminalization of social and political life has become another distinct sign of the crisis. Protection rackets (*reket*), popular throughout Russia in the 1990s (see, e.g., Humphrey 2018; Ledeneva 1998, 2014), resurfaced in Dagestan in a new "Islamic" form. Dues were extracted not in return for "protection" but to "support jihad" (*zakat* for jihad), with the preferred method of extortion being the delivery of a USB flash drive containing a demand for payment, under threat of death or destruction of the victim's property. Protection rackets were run by militants (reket was a significant source of funding for underground organizations) as well as criminals. The victims of these schemes were typically shopkeepers—especially those who sell liquor—government officials, and wealthy businessmen who have been branded *kafirs* (unbelievers). Another increasingly common practice involved paying militants for "protection"; some politicians have retained such services in order to protect their lives and property. Protection rackets became less frequent after 2014, and as one informant, an employee of an Islamic shop in Makhachkala, claimed in

2019, "the state has taken over their role tormenting petty traders with taxes they can't afford."

Although racketeering and the open conflict, rampant at the time of my research, have gradually waned in severity, what has changed little since 2009–2010 is the loss of confidence in the ruling elites and security forces who are perceived as acting to the detriment of society. The "fight against terrorism" waged (with varying intensity) by the security forces at the local and federal levels is seen no longer as an effort to instill order but as a source of the blind violence that affects many residents of Dagestan (discussed in chapter 2). Dagestanis continue to perceive the state as predatory, corrupt, and unable to resolve disputes impartially. Although corruption and nepotism are present at all levels and many common citizens profit from it (Kaliszewska and Schmidt 2022), it is mainly local government officials who are perceived as dishonest and representing the interests of their own clans or the ruling elites, who shared clan ties. This perception is amplified by everyday corruption: state-paid jobs, in particular those at the higher level, are bought and sold (the initial payment is later reclaimed in bribes or kickbacks taken from clients or those lower in hierarchy) and are often viewed purely as a source of official and unofficial income; students pay for exams throughout their university education; in hospitals, up-front payment is invariably demanded for operations and tests; even adoptions are conducted through unofficial means—a child can be bought from its biological mother and registered as the son or daughter of the adopting parents. Overall, public institutions are no longer perceived as public but rather as quasi-private enterprises whose employees need to be paid for their services. As a result, the state has lost its significance as a point of reference or a basis of identity for the local population.

Origins of the Political and Social Instability in Dagestan

Many analyses and newspaper articles trace the political and social turbulence in the North Caucasus to poverty and unemployment, but as I try to demonstrate, these factors are overestimated. The key causes of the social and political instability are the peripheralization of the region, the actions of local elites, shifts in the social structure of the republic's population, the violence of the security apparatus (discussed in chapter 2), and the Kremlin's reactive politics.

In order to understand the structural causes of the political and social instability in Dagestan, we must first take a broader look at the transitions that have occurred in the region over the past several decades, particularly the modernization processes that were conducted under the Soviet Union and cut short by the collapse of the empire. Like other parts of the North Caucasus, Dagestan was drawn into the orbit of Russian influence in the nineteenth century, following the end of the Russo-Persian War of 1804–1813. Despite the highlanders' resistance to the forced imposition of a state system, the region was somewhat integrated with the empire's broader sociopolitical system.[4] Russia built roads, factories, and railroads and established cities and ports (including the current capital), as well as hospitals and secular schools. The Russian language became increasingly common in the public sphere, replacing Arabic (the language used by the intelligentsia and the dominant written language) and Kumyk, the lingua franca of the lowlands. Efforts were made to replace sharia and customary law with Russian law. Regardless of how we assess the actions of imperial Russia in the North Caucasus and whether we describe them as colonization, it remains true that at the social level, the region underwent tremendous modernization, and the process was continued with even greater vigor under Soviet rule. The forced modernization of the 1920s and 1930s, which included the secularization of schools, the shuttering of mosques, and the abolishing of Koranic schools and sharia courts[5] met with resistance that was often brutally suppressed. With time, however, modernization processes became increasingly voluntary, especially in the period after Stalinism. A growing number of Dagestanis identified with the Soviet state, contributed to it, and participated in it.

The collapse of the USSR came as a surprise to most Soviet citizens, including those living in the North Caucasus, where there were few dissidents or people who aspired to independence. The disintegration of the state was, for many people, a life-shattering catastrophe that stripped them of their jobs, social status, and wealth and forced them to quickly regain their bearings in a completely new reality. The decline of the USSR also marked the end of the Soviet modernization campaign. Most of the efforts to integrate the region with the rest of the country were aborted. Impoverished, unstable, and racked by internal conflict, the peripheral regions were abandoned by many Russians, particularly the technical and managerial staff of failing companies; the education system disintegrated as well. Like many other constituents of the newly established Russian Federation, Dagestan was left to fend for itself. The authorities of the republic had to tackle emerging problems on their own. Numerous national movements emerged, none of which garnered significant support, and occasional land disputes erupted and were stoked by slogans echoing the histories of particular ethnic groups. However, these conflicts were resolved without bloodshed. In the political arena, a person's association with a particular jamaat (here, community)[6] was and is more important than their ethnicity, particularly if that jamaat played a foundational role in shaping the Dagestani political scene and the Dagestani elite in the 1990s.

The wars waged in Chechnya in 1994–1996 and 1999–2005, along with the republic's quasi-independence between 1996 and 1999,[7] only exacerbated the crisis in neighboring Dagestan. The republic was plagued by enormous corruption and pervasive crime—including the trafficking of humans, arms, and drugs—resulting in the progressing disintegration of the region from the rest of the country. In 1999, Chechnya-based militants invaded Dagestan with the goal of establishing an Islamic state in the republic. The residents of Dagestan sided with the federal forces, repelling the attack. The event provided the casus belli for the Second Chechen War. Although the ensuing conflict deepened Dagestan's isolation, it also marked the ascension to power of a new Russian leader, Vladimir Putin, who presented himself as strong and uncompromising and who many people hoped would restore law and order in the region.

Even though Putin's rule brought economic improvement—a result of a boom in oil and natural gas prices on international commodity markets—it also resulted in the curtailment of political activity at the local level.[8] A local elite began to cement in Dagestan, supported financially and militarily by the Kremlin[9] in return for its loyalty and rejection of separatist ambitions. An increasingly powerful and pathological system of dependence emerged between the central government in Moscow, the commanders of the security forces, and local authorities. The last of the three were, and continue to be, connected by a web of loyalties rooted in business, clanship, and family. They did not (and do not) provide much to the residents of the republic in terms of public services, education, or health care (Derluguian 2005). Local elites may be described as irresponsible: they are focused on their own particularist interests and loyalties, with little concern for the rest of the citizenry, whom they need neither as recruits, as Dagestan has no external threats, nor as constituents (compare, with regard to the Caucasus as a whole, Derluguian 2005), as elections have been successfully rigged for years, nor as taxpayers, as the elite derive their income from the distribution of federal funding and from the republic's key industries. Economic activity is polarized. On one end are large companies, most of which are controlled by individuals with ties to elites in other parts of the Russian Federation, and sometimes in what is known as the near abroad, meaning the Commonwealth of Independent States (CIS). On the other end are small operations run by individual households, such as family businesses, taxis, car washes, and bars. Instability, the war in neighboring Chechnya, and the lack of prospects drove many people out of Dagestan, not just Russians,[10] but also the intellectual elites and skilled technical workers.

Highly educated individuals and specialists in various fields left the republic and were replaced by Dagestanis from former Soviet states such as Uzbekistan, Turkmenistan, and Georgia, along with people from rural areas, who migrated in large numbers to the cities, particularly the capital, in search of work. As a result of these processes, many of the inhabitants of Dagestan now belong to a large and, to certain extent, ungovernable group of people from rural areas who often lack privileges and influence (but not necessarily money that comes from unreported income). By contrast, there is a dearth of people who would pursue the institutionalization of common goals within the structures of the state, preferring organized long-term competition. George Derluguian (2005) classifies the places in which one observes the above phenomena as the periphery, referencing Immanuel Wallerstein's world-systems theory. He emphasizes that it is not the area's peripheral geographical location that is significant but the relation between the elites and the rest of society, and the degree to which both parties are "disengaged" from the state. Dagestan and many other constituents of the Russian Federation—in the North Caucasus and elsewhere—are examples of such places.

To integrate the North Caucasus with the rest of the Russian Federation, the Kremlin announced in 2010 a social and economic development strategy for the region. At the time, television broadcasts from the North Caucasus were little more than strings of crime reports interrupted with advertisements selling visions of the region's glorious future. Interspersed between coverage of the latest bombing, special forces operation, and assassination were presentations of ambitious plans for the development of the North Caucasian Federal District: thriving factories, ski resorts, and tourism infrastructure. The social and economic development strategy was an attempt to address what the authorities believe to be the causes of the political and social instability in the North Caucasus. According to its creators, the crisis in the region—particularly its most conspicuous manifestation, militant activity—was rooted in economic underdevelopment, unemployment, and poverty. Five years later, in 2015, the plan to "fight radicalism with economic development" had produced little more that weathered billboards on deserted lots, promising a Côte d'Azur on the Caspian Sea.

According to official statistics, Dagestan is indeed one of the poorest constituents of the Russian Federation,[11] with one of the lowest average per capita incomes in the country. To the outside observer, however, the quality of life of the average Dagestani does not differ significantly from that of his or her counterpart in many other parts of the Russian Federation (Falkowski and Marszewski 2010). A significant increase in the number of automobiles, the popularity of expensive home cinema systems, a boom in home renovation, and

Figure 1.2. Solutions to housing problems in the Dagestan capital. Photo by Iwona Kaliszewska.

the influx of cheap foreign labor (mainly construction workers from Vietnam and China) testify to the growing incomes of various strata of the population. Many Dagestanis are involved in trade and have established small businesses, while others work in agriculture; the incomes of many families are further boosted by remittances from seasonal migration to larger cities in the Russian Federation, particularly Moscow and Saint Petersburg, as well as the Russian North (Karpov and Kapustina 2011). The disprivileged or otherwise excluded from the market escape poverty by benefiting from an extensive system of aid to poorer *tukhum* members. In fact, one might argue that contrary to the official statistics, the average resident of Dagestan enjoys a higher quality of life than does a resident of rural Russia. What these statistics fail to consider, however, is Dagestan's highly developed informal economy: there is a significant gap between the official incomes of Dagestanis and their expenditures and living standards. It is estimated that half of the Dagestani gross domestic product comes from unofficial incomes, nonlegalized trade, and corruption.[12] The significance of economic factors in tracing the roots of political and social unrest, in particular radicalism seems, therefore, severely overstated. Rather, the sociopolitical transitions I described in this chapter, along with the state violence I discuss in chapter 2, laid fertile ground for the radicalization of young people seeking order and social justice.

CHAPTER 2

Torture, Exorcisms, and Checkpoints
Experiencing the "Fight against Terrorism"

The majority of the inhabitants of Dagestan remain outside the conflict between the militants fighting under the banner of Islam and the Russian state—the Ministry of Internal Affairs (MVD) and Federal Security Service of the Russian Federation (FSB)—yet the violence, regardless of its source, permeates their everyday lives and is consequently internalized, thus becoming a familiar part of their world. It is not always articulated but is expressed through a variety of means and in various places, shaping the way people perceive the state and its agents.

In this chapter, I demonstrate how the "fight against terrorism" is experienced by Dagestanis and how this experience shapes the image of the state. I explore the experiences of Dagestani Muslims with regard to the conflict and the fight against terrorism currently under way. I show that when one lives in a place where violence affects many aspects of one's everyday life, where specific places serve as reminders of this violence and where one avoids encounters with law enforcement officers, the state—when viewed in light of the actions of its agents—begins to manifest itself as the source of unwarranted violence. At the rhetorical level, the actions undertaken by the security apparatus are rationalized as a fight against terrorism, yet in places where these efforts are carried out and where these rules of the game apply, the legitimacy of the state deteriorates, and its agents are perceived not as law enforcement officers but rather as sources of violence, chaos, and lawlessness. Experiences of this type do not prevent people from viewing in a positive light the abstract state, an entity that is separate from the practices of its local agents. On the one hand, the state—when perceived through the lens of everyday experiences and encounters with its local agents—is seen as a source of unwarranted violence, conflicts, and crisis. Yet, the actual idea of the state (to borrow Abrams's term[1]) as an abstract force, an autonomous agent personified by Putin, Stalin, or Lenin, is evaluated positively; the actions of the abstract state are rationalized and seen as warranted. The reified state survives deconstruction; there are, however, ruptures and frictions ahead, which I discuss in later in this book.

My Encounter with the State

Violence had been a part of the lives of my interviewees long before I first took note of this aspect of their world. I had read about murders, persecution, and tortures on the website of the organization Memorial,[2] and I had heard heartrending stories, yet I was incapable of comprehending the violence without at least a tiny sample of my interviewees' experiences. Without my encounters with the state, from which I luckily emerged unscathed by physical violence but which exposed me to plenty of symbolic violence, it would have been difficult for me to convey many experiences, to fully empathize with people's fear, indignation, and their contempt for the agents of the state.

At a certain point, visits to police stations, local offices of the FSB, and GAI (State Automobile Inspectorate) checkpoints[3] became a constant element of my fieldwork. I never experienced the hell of a detention center, but I did walk down corridors where any door could have led to a torture chamber. I listened carefully. I saw terror in the eyes of people awaiting "sentencing" by a police or FSB chief; I saw the intimidating faces of the employees of these institutions, any of whom could have been a potential oppressor. A sour-faced plainclothes officer threatened to call in an OMON team if I refused to accompany him to an FSB office; I was driven to a police station in the back seat of a bulletproof *uazik*.[4] I was detained for long hours of questioning, during which I had to prove that I was not a spy, that I had not come to distribute money to Wahhabis, and that I worked for neither the Gosdep (U.S. State Department) nor a certain English nongovernmental organization that had been depicted in a propaganda film as providing aid to Dagestani militants. I was forced to show the pictures on my camera, lie, hide recordings of interviews, and conceal information about the people who talked to me and showed me hospitality. I felt fear and contempt for the men who were questioning me. Bundled with these emotions was a sense of anger and helplessness. One Dagestani acquaintance in his mid-thirties, with whom I was once picked up by the FSB, introduced me to the tactics involved in talking to members of the security apparatus, admonishing me for my insolence and lack of respect. "You have to understand, these people have blood on their hands. They're capable of anything. Don't talk to them that way. You'll thank me for that advice." This was after I had refused to allow an agent at a local FSB office to copy the photos I had on my camera on the grounds that they were my private property (the actual reason was to prevent the images of people I had talked to from falling into the hands of the FSB). "But I'll tell you one thing, if they keep being this disrespectful, they're not going to live long. The locals won't stand for it," he added with disgust.

The frequency of my encounters with government agents intensified between 2008 and 2010. I gradually became more proficient in interpreting the hierarchies of power. I learned, for example, that just a bit of impertinence or the mention of (real or fabricated) personal connections was enough to dissuade a low-level cop from taking me in for questioning. When, in 2010, two friends and I were stopped by three rank-and-file officers who claimed that we had to be taken to the police station to be registered, I replied that we were tired and hungry and that we had to go home, not to the police station. They insisted, arguing that it was in the interest of our own safety. "It seems to me that we'll be safer at home than with you," I remarked, alluding to the attacks on the police that were a frequent occurrence at the time. I stressed that we were very hungry and that I would consider them inhospitable if they did not permit us, foreigners, to eat. As I said this, I pointed to my friends, whom I had previously instructed to pretend not to understand Russian so that they would appear truly foreign in the eyes of law enforcement officers (and thus avoid additional questioning). Appeals to hospitality and personal connections were typically effective against low-ranking police officers and traffic inspectors, but tactics of this type were useless against the FSB and higher-ranking employees of the MVD. In such situations, I had to learn to hide my anger and refrain from appealing to higher authorities, for example by threatening to phone the embassy. I knew that if I behaved inappropriately, I could end up hurting myself and my interviewees. With this in mind, I made an effort to take the officers' questions seriously and refrained from answering questions about cash for Wahhabis in the tone I had sometimes used previously: "Sure, I've got a backpack full of dollars and three grenade launchers." When they asked if I had come as a spy, I no longer replied, "You got me. I've counted every last sheep in the region." Whenever I traveled (or did anything else that increased the likelihood of my being detained), I made a point of removing the SD card from my camera and replacing it with one filled with landscape shots (though this likely did more harm than good when, before one interrogation in 2008, I swapped out the card for one that had nothing but pictures of the donkeys that roamed the local hillsides). I also understood that when Dagestanis were arrested or brought in for questioning, their experiences were nothing like my adventures with the security services. For example, instead of inquiring about what I was doing there, the Russian soldiers manning the checkpoints and patrolling the borders would joke and ask me if I had Russian roots (I did not always disabuse them of this idea). In contrast, local men would not only have their documents checked but also their faces and hands (which were inspected for the callouses typically left on the fingers by automatic rifles). Dagestani security forces officers were impolite and suspicious of me; however, they were also compelled by their strongly internalized rules of hospitality to treat foreigners (especially women) differently than they would a random local man. Additionally, foreigners were such a rare occurrence that sometimes the officials would feel lost. "Now you deal with them since you brought them here. And you do the writing," I overheard at the police station in Botlikh where, together with two of my friends, we were detained for six hours. Completing the paperwork was no easy task since none of the policemen present knew how to read the Latin alphabet in our passports.

Eventually, I also came to understand why the very mention of a police station (*mentovka*), the Regional Department of Internal Affairs (ROVD), also referred to as *mentovki*, or the FSB would bring up memories of fear and violence for my interviewees. I gradually internalized this sense of fear, which could then be evoked by a growing number of stories, places, and associations. I was also increasingly fearful, sometimes to the point of paranoia, of being detained again; I changed my phone number constantly, hoping to evade the wiretaps about which I had been warned, and I paid more attention to the way I dressed, making sure to choose outfits that were as inconspicuous as possible. These experiences helped me to better understand the people whom I interviewed, to immerse myself in the experience of their traumatic encounters with the state, to fully comprehend their fear of violence.

The Fight against Terrorism in Dagestan: From Faraway War to the Experience of Violence

Stories involving "counterterrorism" operations came up frequently in the interviews I conducted in 2005–2009. The violence recounted in these testimonies was a part of everyday life in Makhachkala, yet it was not initially part of my own experience, nor was it experienced directly by the people I interviewed.

The security services were widely mocked for their lack of professionalism and training. Residents of the city were annoyed by the endless traffic jams caused by the operations of law enforcement agencies, and they sympathized with those whose property was destroyed in their raids. Violence was present in these stories, yet it was somehow distant: it was not "our conflict"; it was going on "somewhere far away." One interviewee, a man in his mid-forties, recalled an event that took place in his neighborhood in the northern part of the city:

> There was this special operation some time ago. They pulled up in BTRs [armored personnel carriers] with all their heavy artillery and opened fire at a building. They surrounded the house. People started gathering to see what was going on, and the police weren't able to keep the onlookers away from the scene. "Over there! Shoot him! Wrong side! To the right!" someone yelled. A bunch of young men were cheering for the shooters: "Look at the window! Over there! He's peeking out!" In the end, it turned out that two siloviki were killed and the militants managed to escape the siege.... It's a joke. That's how these special operations turn out here.

In 2005–2009, I was not able to track down a single person who claimed to support the insurgency; fearful of sharing their views in the face of the powerful anti-Wahhabi rhetoric of the time, people like them retreated into the shadows or disappeared from public life altogether.

As time went by, I observed a distinct shift in the way my interviewees perceived the actions of the security services and the militants. The faraway war, present in the form of shootings and explosions, grew closer; the stories behind government operations were more frequently revealed, and it became increasingly apparent that the violence and torture were linked to the bureaucracy and corruption.

The narratives of the conflict and violence began to change gradually after 2009. I heard more and more stories of violence and could sense a mounting disdain for the operations of both the militant underground and the state. "They'll shell a single apartment for three days straight," one acquaintance, in his forties, told me, alluding to one of the many special operations that had been conducted in his neighborhood. "Who knows if there were any militants there to begin with? They get paid by the hour for KTOs [counterterrorism operations], so it's worth their while to fight as long as possible. They can always find some militants later. And the commander earns his stripes." It is also noteworthy that narratives featuring the detonation of explosives, while more spectacular, appeared less frequently and had a shorter shelf life (possibly due to the fact that such events were less likely to affect family members, as civilians were not targeted by militants). Meanwhile, narratives and conversations involving the counterterrorism operations conducted by the state became an everyday occurrence.

More and more of my interviewees expressed their doubts about the intentions of the state. "They'll claim those men were militants again," one woman in her thirties remarked, sadly, when the driver of our marshrutka informed his passengers that four men had been killed in the shooting we had just heard and which had been the cause of a traffic jam. Jibrail, sixty-seven years old, recalled his encounter with a counterterrorist unit in Makhachkala in 2013:

> They started pounding on my door. I opened it, and there was a counterterrorist unit. "We have a warrant ordering you to vacate the premises. There are militants in the building across the street," they said. "We have to keep them under surveillance." "I'm not going anywhere," I said. But you know how it is: they'll plant a grenade or drugs. So I told my wife to hurry up and pack our valuables and go stay with her family, and I would stay home. They moved the couch and the desk and lay on the floor with their guns, aiming through the balcony door. "You're aiming at the wrong apartment! An old lady lives in that one!" I said, politely. "Do you even know what you're doing? Don't aim at that one—my niece and her kids live there!" I said somewhat less politely. They yelled at me to shut up, and they just kept watching the building across the street, all tense. They lay there for three hours, all agitated, and finally they were ordered to retreat. That evening we found out that the people living in the building across the street had seen three bodies in the stairwell. Their theory was that the bodies were planted: those boys didn't even live there, nobody had ever seen them. A typical story in Dagestan.

Throughout the course of my fieldwork, year by year, death and violence gradually became more familiar, more tangible. Abstract-sounding narratives turned into stories about relatives, neighbors, and classmates. Violence would erupt unexpectedly: it was unanticipated and difficult to pinpoint in the ostensibly normal everyday life of the Dagestani capital. What became much more apparent was the connection between the shootings I regularly heard and the kidnappings, tortures, and murders that were occurring. More and more frequently, my interviewees would recount, often in hushed tones, the stories of boys, alleged militants killed in special operations; stories about (often innocent) people who had simply found themselves in the wrong place at the wrong time or helped the wrong person, for instance by lending a car to a friend or relative with ties to underground groups. Detained by unidentified masked men (who would pull up in unmarked cars at dawn or in the middle of the night), they would be interrogated at the ROVD and tortured into signing false confessions. The bodies of those who did not survive the torture would be planted, along with a Kalashnikov rifle, at the sites of special operations. They would be "eliminated" (*likvidirovani*, a term used by the media) in the fight against terrorism.

The following is an excerpt of the field journal I kept in 2010 and 2011. I contacted Mariam, a woman in her early thirties who worked as a music teacher in Kaspiysk, hoping that she could help me get in touch with colleagues or neighbors who had recently turned to Islam.

"I'm not in touch with people who escaped into religion." Mariam did not like my question.

"What about your cousin Zumrut? She wears the hijab, doesn't she?" Mariam's mother Leila, in her late fifties, joined the conversation.

"I don't know anyone named Zumrut," Mariam replied.

"Sure you do. The one whose husband they killed last month."

We meet Zumrut not far from the carpenter's shop where she works.[5] Zumrut is about twenty-five years old. She is dressed in work clothes and has specks of sawdust on her hijab. Her husband Murat ran his own home renovation company, driving around Makhachkala in a car that belonged to Zumrut's brother. Murat didn't come home one night. The next day Zumrut and her father were brought in for questioning at the ROVD. Investigators asked her about her husband and brother. She was forced to sign a document stating that her husband was involved with an underground Islamist organization, even though she knew he had nothing to do with the group.

Following extensive questioning, Zumrut was taken to the basement of the detention center, where she was shown her husband's mutilated body. They told her that he had been attempting to plant an explosive device on train tracks when it exploded in his hands. The body bore clear signs of torture, cuts, and burns. Zumrut was horrified and nearly collapsed. She wasn't able to take her husband's body home right away. "If they say the device exploded in his hands, how could he possibly have cuts on his body? Why were his legs damaged?" she later wondered. "At least they released his body," Leila added, breaking the awkward silence. It is not uncommon in the North Caucasus for the family to be deprived of the right to even give a proper burial to a relative who is believed to have been a terrorist. The unofficial payment demanded for the release of a body is about seventy thousand rubles. Officers at the ROVD instructed Zumrut to bury her husband's remains as soon as possible, in keeping with Islamic customs. She suspected, however, that their true intent was to avoid further investigation and to cover up evidence of the events that regularly took place in detention centers.

Zumrut's house was searched while she was at the ROVD. A scanner, camera, printer, and the gold jewelry given to her as a wedding present by her husband's family were taken. Zumrut never reported this to the court, as she considered any interaction with the authorities to be pointless. She could easily prove that Murat had died in result of torture, but she made no efforts to seek justice. "I don't want to have to look at their ugly mugs or have anything to do with them. They'll pay for what they've done. Their punishment will come from Allah," Zumrut said with contempt. "And my son is growing up . . . ," she added. Leila sympathized with Zumrut and, like her, spoke about the "scum" in the detention centers and counterterrorist units with scorn.

When I returned home, I looked up the circumstances surrounding Murat's death. I read that the police had succeeding in thwarting the attack. According to sources in the MVD, "the suicide bomber was killed when he accidentally detonated the explosive device." This was most likely the version that was officially filed.

Zumrut was not informed about the proceedings of Murat's case. A perfunctory investigation may have been conducted. Murat's forced testimonies were all the "credible evidence" the court needed. The case was quickly closed.

In March 2011, one year after my conversation with Zumrut, I sat down with Mariam's family to watch television. It was the one-year anniversary of the 2010 Moscow metro bombings, and Vladimir Putin was in the news, explaining the urgency of the fight against terrorists, and saying that all hotbeds of terrorism in the North Caucasus needed to be eliminated. "He's absolutely right! The terrorists must be destroyed!" Leila commented.

After dinner, I asked Leila about Zumrut. She told me that Zumrut's brother had recently been killed and that this time the body had not been released. "If they didn't release the body, then maybe that means he really was a militant? I heard them say on TV that they don't release the bodies of militants," she added.

The kinds of torture suffered by people like Murat have become a widespread method of coercing confessions in the entire North Caucasus (Kvedaravičius 2008; Raubisko 2012).[6] Electric shocks, nail pulling, and rape with a truncheon are just some of the methods used to get a "standard suspect" to admit his "standard guilt"—typically membership in an informal militant organization (*neformalnye band-formiraniya*). An admission of guilt has become the crowning evidence that allows authorities to close a case without conducting a proper investigation or questioning witnesses. Cases that remain open are informally referred to hangers (*veshalki*). They are often closed by pinning (hanging) them on innocent people who have been forced into making confessions, often through the use of torture. Cases like these are considered a job well done, evidence that the members of the government apparatus are as professional as they claim to be in the reports touting their diligence, meticulousness, and efficacy in fighting terrorists. Torture and confessions used as incontrovertible evidence of a crime have thus become more than just a technique: they are a routine and repeatable bureaucratic practice, one that is theoretically independent of those by whom it is implemented. Investigators and ROVD staff resort to torture as a widely accepted practice and not, as one might expect, as a method used deliberately in special circumstances. In this sense, they are no different from other everyday routine practices. The use of torture is rarely the result of any devious strategy; it is a mindlessly repeated practice that is not subjected to reflection. Any responsibility is shifted onto the torturer's superiors (Raubisko 2012).

Violence, however, does not exist in the abstract: there are only individuals, agents of the state who act as perpetrators of unwarranted violence with the ostensible goal of upholding the law (the effectiveness of this violence, as Walter Benjamin shows, gives the established legal order the appearance of permanence[7]). Lawlessness is legitimized by appealing to the law: it requires nothing more than the proper testimonies and paperwork.

Such practices as extracting confessions by torture and murdering people to achieve the desired statistics have a long history in Russia. They are a product of the statistical management model developed in the USSR, a system that revolved around the idea of central planning in which the final results were determined at the start, and thus the way in which these statistics were presented was sometimes more important than the manner in which they were achieved. Bureaucracy ballooned as the Soviet state underwent rapid modernization. In the period of the Great Terror (1937–1938), the bureaucratic apparatus of the state was so overwhelmed by the sheer number of arrestees that authorities often resorted to beating and torture in order to coerce suspects into admitting their guilt. To increase the efficiency of the system, teams were set up with one or two People's Commissariat for Internal Affairs (NKVD) agents, a prosecutor, and the local party secretary; known as troikas, these three-person commissions issued sentences, include death sentences, following hasty investigations held behind closed doors, often without the presence of the accused. To them, a confession was worth more than proof of guilt. What mattered was that the troika carried out their orders, which meant extracting testimonies proving that the suspect had committed the crime in question, without which the interrogator could be sanctioned by his superior for missing his quota. Whether the person was actually guilty of any crime was beside the point.[8]

The prevalence and sociopolitical causes of such practices are different today than they were under Stalinism, yet some similarities can be observed in the patterns by which state institutions operate. The fight against terrorism demands fast results, ones that lower-level agents, fearing the loss of their jobs, are willing to achieve through a variety of means, with the tacit approval of their superiors, who may themselves be angling for a promotion (Solonenko and Karpov 2011).

In Dagestan and the broader North Caucasus, the fight against terrorism is an umbrella concept encompassing a number of local practices that have little resemblance to popular media representations of the global war on terror (or perhaps, this war comprises similar practices rooted in local contexts). These practices are deeply rooted in the social and historical contexts of the region, including the symbiotic coupling of violence and bureaucracy inherent in the Russian system of rule.

Under these circumstances, there occurred over the course of several years a gradual shift in the public perception of the actions of government officials, who came to be seen as the sources of violence—the kind that is meted out mindlessly, often blindly, and is motivated by bureaucratic concerns or simple greed but also intentional violence geared toward the elimination of "terrorists," a label that can be applied indiscriminately. No longer regarded as trustworthy people, local government officials became potential murderers whom one had to be wary of and to whom human life was practically worthless.

The Fight against Terrorism as an Embodied Conflict

Detention and arrest were not the only circumstances in which people feared for their lives and the lives of their loved ones. Violence becomes inscribed in the bodies and minds of the people for whom fear is an inherent part of everyday life (Trigg 2012).

The following is an edited excerpt from the field journal I kept in 2010.

The Story of Amina: Conflicts in the Body

Amina was suffering from depression. She was in her late thirties and had a husband and two boys. She had been having headaches and trouble sleeping. She wasn't getting along with her husband: she wanted him to pray and be a "true" (*istinniy*) Muslim, like she was. "I have a neighbor who mutters under her breath whenever she sees me: 'I hate those Muslims!' Maybe she was the one who put a curse [*zglaz*] on me," wondered Amina. She had seen doctors, but none of them were able to help her. Finally, someone recommended Abdul-Hamid, who told her that she might be possessed by a jinn that was causing her health problems.

"Here, put this on. It's necessary," Amina said, handing me a hijab. After a moment she lay down on the floor and covered herself with a blue fleece blanket. She gave me the sign to call in Abdul-Hamid.

Abdul-Hamid hadn't even had time to prepare for the prayer when Amina's entire body began to tremble.

"Oh, here we go, it's starting," the exorcist said.[9] He began to read surahs from the Quran in Arabic, switching to Russian every now and again: "Begone, enemy of Allah! Begone! Begone, enemy of Allah!"

"I hate you, *yedinobozhniki*!"[10] shouted a voice from inside Amina.[11]

"Why did you enter her?"

"It's what I had to do."

"Do you not fear the Creator? Nor the day of judgment? You will appear before him! Become a *yedinobozhnik*!" Abdul-Hamid yelled, hitting Amina's body with a miswak stick, a teeth-cleaning twig made from the wood of the arak tree.

"I've had enough of her *yedinobozhiye*. I'm sick of it!"

"What is your name?"

"Igor!"

"Igor? Are you Christian? Where are you hiding? I'm going to blow now. I'll find you with the help of Allah. Begone!"

"She'll choke to death! *Adufff, tiiliriri prifu, bll,* leave me be! Leave me be! Why do you hate me?"

"Where did you come from?"

"They sent me."

"Where from?"

"Makhachkala One.[12] I sat behind the icon of St. Peter in the church in Makhachkala."

"Are you Christian?"

"Of course I am. What are you, some kind of idiot?"

"Do you believe in God? You know you can't do things like this. . . ."[13]

"And who am I supposed to say that to? Who am I supposed to lead down the wrong path? Those idiots who come to light those candles, to keep us warm?"

"They keep you warm? Why are you doing this? What are you doing this for?" Abdul-Hamid asks.

"Muslims . . . I'm going to lead Muslims down the wrong path. Why do you think I entered Amina's body? Kill her. I have to kill her."

"Is that your purpose? Your goal?"

"She's a *yedinobozhnitsa*. I have to kill her. We don't touch *Sufiki* [members of Sufi orders]. There was a *Sufik* in her body, Mahmud was his name. . . . There were so many of them."

"Do you know that you will stand before God? . . . Can you translate these words: *La ilaha illa-llah?*" Abdul-Hamid asks.

"The true religion of Allah is Islam."

"Do you deny that? You know it's Islam and yet you fight[14] it?" Abdul-Hamid asks.

"Learn how to talk! Learn how to speak Russian!"

"I'm not Russian [*russkiy*]. I'm from Dagestan," Abdul-Hamid says.

"You're kidding."

"What did they promise in return for rejecting your faith? Why are you doing this?"

"I fear the sorcerer."

"Why do you fear the sorcerer? It's Allah you should fear."

"I don't understand all of this. My brain isn't what it should be. I don't understand yedinobozhiye."

"How old are you?"

"Two hundred and fifty. I'm still young. I'm going to live another three thousand years."

"How do you know that?"

"Every jinn lives to be three to five thousand years old. Three is short. Satan has a thousand years of experience in deceiving people. He tricked the Jews and the Christians. The Jews tricked the Christians because Christians are stupid. . . . And those yedinobozhniki, I'm sick of them, we're fighting them; we've got a whole army on the ground and in the sky."

"And yet there are more and more of us. You can never destroy the love of Allah."

"And you—why did you come to her? I'm not afraid of you," the jinn says.

"There's no reason to fear me."

"I'm afraid of that old man with the beard, so spiky." *Mashallah*.[15]

"He is terrible to behold."

"You're afraid of his beard? See, that's a sunnah."

"Go say your prayers! Perform your namaz! Leave me alone! Everyone's ganging up on me. There's no need to read those surahs."

"*Ahad ahad* . . . Oh, the *adhan*. It's the call to prayer," Abdul-Hamid says, turning to me. We hear the muezzin calling from the mosque.

"Why don't you suffer without me," he says to the jinn.

"See, he doesn't like the adhan," Abdul-Hamid explains to me as he gets up and leaves the room to pray.

The ritual is over. Amina signals for us to stop. She asks the men to leave but gestures for me to stay.

Amina takes her prayer rug and starts to pray. She is calm but too exhausted to reflect on what she has just experienced. She does not recall Igor or any other part of the above conversation. She only briefly mentions her hateful Russian neighbor and her curse. She asks me how it went; I struggle to find the right word and finally settle on "powerful." I do not know what to make of Amina's possession. Is possession, as Janice Boddy (1994) suggests, the hold exerted over human beings by more powerful external entities? Was Amina given the scope during the reading to recontextualize the experiences of fear and humiliation that she was facing as a Salafi-oriented Muslim and as a wife of a nonobservant and indifferent husband? Did the exorcism help her expand and regenerate her senses of self?

Embodied Conflicts and Memories of the Flesh

Abdul-Hamid's dialogue with the jinn exposes a host of social problems: from the persecution of Muslims by government officials ("we've got a whole army on the ground and in the sky") and the preferential treatment of Sufi order members (derisively called Sufiki) by the authorities, to the military superiority of the Kremlin and Russian power structures, which favor violent means of conflict resolution, and the overall dominance of Russians and the Russian language. The conflict in Dagestan, the fear of violence, complex social relations, and unequal power relations were all played out in Amina's body. According to Michel Foucault, hegemony leaves its mark on the body: illnesses and other diseases can reflect broader forms of social injustice (cited in Scheper-Hughes and Lock 1987). Spirits can also enter into complex, partially mimetic relations with communities and history (see, for example, the discussion of sub-Saharan Africa in Lambek 1981). A community can go as far as to construct its own pantheon of spirits that reflects and processes the history of interethnic contact and social hierarchies (see, for example, Lambek 1993).

We can thus view Amina's possession as the embodiment of hegemonic discourses and state practices such as the fight against terrorism. Her possession, her body, and what was happening within it revealed her sense of victimhood: she saw herself as a victim of chaos and of a state that is perceived as a source of violence. Her misfortune is caused by a "whole army of devils on the ground and in the sky." Pinpointing the reasons for the misfortunes that befall an individual may help order that person's world, make events more bearable, and shift the guilt onto external forces (Herzfeld 2016). As the exchange cited above suggests, jinns can deploy a "whole army" to fight yedinobozhniki,[16] who are more susceptible to violence than are members of Sufi orders (who are considered loyal within these rhetorical divisions).

The existence of "memories of the flesh" (see, for example, Trigg 2012) and memories of fear and violence does not necessarily mean that people can only be passive recipients of violence. They can also serve as places of resistance against the social labels ascribed to them (Nguyen and Peschard 2003), including such classifications as terrorist. Wielding the Koran in a fight against the jinn offers hope of victory in more than just the struggle with the illness. Abdul-Hamid reaffirms in the jinn the belief that against all odds, the number of yedinobozhniki is rising and that no one can defeat the faith of Allah. The ritual of chasing out the jinn restores meaning: it strengthens the participants' faith in the value of yedinobozhiye and in their own powers: "There are more and more of us! You cannot defeat us." It is a form of empowerment in the face of fear and potential persecution. This is because the human body is not merely a passive recipient of violence. It can serve as the location of budding resistance, sparked by practices that resemble the one described above, ones that can empower individuals and furnish them with counter-hegemonic meanings (Hebdige 1979; cited in Nguyen and Peschard 2003).

We will never know if the ritual actually empowered Amina or allowed her to recontextualize her experiences of fear. Abdul-Hamid has never talked to Igor or any other jinn again. Soon after our encounter, he learned that Islam forbids its followers to engage in conversation with jinns. He later performed exorcisms on Amina and claimed to have cured her. Abdul-Hamid also heard that she had remarried but has since lost touch with her and her family.

Due to the ongoing conflict in Dagestan, many people live in constant (and often unconscious) fear for their own lives and the lives of their close relatives. They internalize the violence. More than just a feature of their everyday lives, it is remembered in the bodies and minds of those who live in constant fear (see, for example, Trigg 2012). They internalize the fear of an unexpected visit by the siloviki, the fear of an UAZ jeep and violence perpetrated by the state, as well as the fear of violence in general, regardless of its source. My interviewees experienced fear in a variety of circumstances, even when traveling outside the Republic of Dagestan, where there was no direct threat, but the "memories of the flesh" remained all the same (Trigg 2012).

Lena, a Dagestani friend of mine in her early forties, came to visit me in Warsaw in December 2010. She was abruptly awoken after dawn by the sound of a garbage truck emptying the bins. "'Oh, another explosion [*vzryv*],' I thought. To hell with them!" she told me the next day. "It took me a moment to realize that I was in Warsaw, not Makhachkala!"

The deeply embodied fear of violence would sometimes manifest itself only after a person had returned to Dagestan after a prolonged absence. Many acquaintances talked about how difficult it was for them to come home after spending as little as a few months outside the republic and how difficult it was for them to readjust to the sounds of gunfire and explosions.

Rumina, aged thirty-eight, who had spent a year in Moscow before returning to Dagestan in 2009, recounted the time she witnessed a shooting as she was taking a marshrutka through the center of Makhachkala. Terrified, she instinctively dropped to the floor. The marshrutka stopped in the middle of Lenin Street (now known as Gamzatov Street). The driver turned off the engine and looked out the window. The other passengers awaited further events with stoic calm, curiosity, or annoyance ("Who knows how long this could take? Is it worth waiting?"). This occurred several months before our conversation. Over time, Rumina claimed, she grew accustomed to such incidents. Even though at first she found them stressful and would listen apprehensively, she eventually stopped noticing the gunshots. Yet, the sense of tension never went away. She considered the possibility of moving to Moscow.

Few of my interviewees spoke as candidly about their fear for their own lives as Rumina did. Most of them assured me that they had gotten "used to it" and that "if it's their turn to die, then there's nothing they can do about it." They talked about methods—persecution, torture—but not about their emotions (this can be explained by local traditions, which require people to restrain expressions of fear). The dread of violence was often hidden much deeper and remained unarticulated; it was remembered "in the body," as were the complex power relations that caused them. It was only when I participated in the exorcism that I realized just how deeply hidden this unarticulated fear of violence could be.

People grow accustomed to the fear of violence: it becomes an integral and inherent part of their everyday lives. Events that evoked fear in me and my companions would simply be shrugged off by locals. Remaining indifferent to such occurrences, not hearing or seeing them, may have served as a defensive strategy of sorts, an attempt to shield one's everyday life or rebuild it with normalized fear and violence as its intrinsic elements.

In March 2010, as I was having my evening tea with a colleague and some Dagestani friends, I heard gunfire outside the window. No one besides the two of us[17] seemed to pay any attention to what had happened. My local friends continued their conversation. They were discussing the possible options for providing aid to single women in Dagestan. "I think I heard gunshots," I remarked. "Yeah, our boys are in town," my interviewee, a woman in her late fifties, laughed, not skipping a beat. As in the case of the inhabitants of the Nicaraguan village described by Aleksandra Pytko (2008) who are inured to the stench of the hydrogen sulfide emitted by the nearby volcano (an odor that eventually became imperceptible to the author herself), it is possible that the inhabitants of Makhachkala are in fact deaf to the gunfire that has become an immanent part of the sonic space of their everyday lives.

The Spatial Experience of Violence: KTO Zones and Checkpoints

The social and political instability in Dagestan and the dread of violence engendered by this struggle have spatial dimensions as well. Checkpoints, borders crossings, and places where counterterrorism operations have been carried out not only become locations marked by violence but also spaces in which such violence is in a sense anticipated.

Places strongly associated with the experience of violence include detention centers and counterterrorism operation (KTO) zones—points and areas that the residents of Dagestan encounter on an everyday basis.

KTO zones, according to the definitions laid out in the 1998 law on the fight against terrorism, are "the particular areas of land or water, vehicles, buildings, structures, installations, or premises and the adjoining territory or waters within which the [counterterrorist] operation is carried out."[18] A counterterrorist operation, meanwhile, is defined as the "special measures aimed at stopping terrorist activities, ensuring the security of individuals, neutralizing terrorists, and also minimizing the consequences of terrorist activities." KTO zones are established in various places and at various times; they pose an obstacle to people coming home from work and expose them to additional searches and the threat of shakedowns; they cause damage to private property. Such places can be said to demarcate the boundaries of the "state emergency" (Benjamin 1968; cited in Raubisko 2012), which at once absorbs and exudes violence (Taussig 2005, 30; Raubisko 2012). Even though legal on the one hand, these zones are, on the other hand, beyond the reach of law and order, and arbitrary means of combating terrorism can be applied within them.

Post-KTO areas, meaning places in which special operations have been conducted, have become a permanent spatial feature of Makhachkala. Tucked between undamaged buildings and hidden behind tall fences, they are not immediately visible. They are often indiscernible from construction sites and buildings that are being torn down to make way for new commercial or residential real estate. Some are present only in stories and accounts.

In October 2010, I made plans with an acquaintance to attend the wedding of one of her work colleagues. I called her up to set a meeting place.

"Let's meet at the corner of Engels and that street that runs down to the market," Lena, a woman in her early forties, suggested.

"Where's that?" I inquired.

"You know, that place I told you about, the one where that special operation happened. Go up by the market and on the right you'll see the house they bombed. You can't miss it: there's an entire floor that's burned out. I'll wait for you across the street."

Violence would reveal itself in places like these, sometimes through subtle traces that were not apparently visible to the untrained eye. It was only after I had spent some time in Makhachkala that I began to notice the bullet holes around the newly installed plastic window frames and renovated balconies, and the burned walls of buildings (see figure 2.1). Other times, all evidence of the special operation had long ceased to exist, but the memory of violence remained. "Make a turn by that store that they burned down; keep going for a bit and you'll find it," one friend explained, giving me directions, even though the torched store had long since been razed and rebuilt and there was no sign that a fire had ever occurred.

The most frequently encountered and most unavoidable places in which violence was experienced or anticipated were the checkpoints. Created in the

46   CHAPTER 2

FIGURE 2.1.   Aftermath of a special operation in downtown Makhachkala. Photo by Iwona Kaliszewska.

Soviet Union as a way of controlling the migration of its citizens, checkpoints now ostensibly serve to increase the security of citizens of the Russian Federation. They are typically found at the outskirts of cities, on thoroughfares leading in and out of town, at the borders of administrative regions, on roads branching off from main routes, at the entrances to tunnels, near hydroelectric dams (Russian: *gidroelektrostantsiya*, commonly referred to as a GES), and other strategic locations. Checkpoints occur in the North Caucasus with much greater frequency than elsewhere in Russia. A typical checkpoint consists of a characteristic guardhouse perched atop a two-story tower or, in the case of minor roadblocks, a small concrete booth resembling Cossack watchtowers (King 2008). A requisite feature of every checkpoint is the boom barrier, which is kept open on heavily frequented roads and closed on smaller ones and is usually accompanied by speed bumps. Major roadblocks are reinforced with sandbags and guarded by policemen and military personnel wearing bulletproof vests, ready to repulse an attack at any moment. The road linking Dagestan and the Stavropol *Krai*, for example, crosses what is in theory an ordinary border, in the middle of the steppe, between two administrative regions of the Russian Federation. Yet, in terms of the number of buildings and fortifications it contains, the thoroughness of the inspections conducted there, and the accompanying level of tension, the checkpoint resembles a well-secured border crossing between two states.

The reasons cited to justify the existence of these checkpoints include the need to decrease levels of violence and to thwart attempts by militants to enter cities. In these locations, the fight against terrorism is conducted by flagging down and inspecting large numbers of vehicles. Yet nearly every checkpoint can be circumvented via local roads, and at each one, travelers can avoid inspections by making the appropriate payment, the price of which is commonly known. Checkpoints were once seen as little more than toll booths where drivers were regularly stopped and almost always shaken down for bribes: fifty to one hundred rubles "for nothing" (in 2010; the price has since increased) and larger payments demanded for minor infractions.[19] They have since acquired a new dimension and can now be described as places in which violence is anticipated in a twofold manner. Not unlike the heavily guarded buildings of important state institutions, checkpoints by their very existence indicate a target, a place that can potentially be attacked. By driving through a checkpoint, one is reminded of the reason why it exists (Jeganathan 2004, 69), of the possibility of an attack or exchange of gunfire. Violence is also anticipated by the soldiers and policemen who staff the checkpoints and inspect the passing people and vehicles.

"If they see a car with shady-looking people inside, they don't pull them over. They just look the other way. They're afraid that someone could open fire and they could get hurt. These people want to live, too. But if they see regular people driving by, they pull them over, because that's always an opportunity for a shakedown," one friend in his forties told me when I asked him about the purpose of checkpoints. These observations were later echoed by a retired policeman in his fifties, who openly admitted that as he approached retirement, he performed his work with less dedication, simply biding his time and securing a proper pension for his wife and children.

In places like Dagestan—unstable areas where attacks and special operations occur frequently—the locations of anticipated violence are constantly moving, shifting with each explosion or threat thereof. Checkpoints are an attempt by the state to control that movement by stating clearly, "This is a target" (Jeganathan 2004, 70). A checkpoint located at the entrance to a city designates that city as a target by standing at its outskirts. Similarly, the masked law enforcement officer standing guard in front of an ordinary building focuses our attention on it, designating it as potential target, a place in which violence can be anticipated. The presence of the state is strongly palpable in such places: the authorities perform their magic, reminding us of their existence and of violence, turning each memory of this violence into a moment of anticipation (72).

In May 2009, I took a marshrutka from Grozny to Makhachkala. Hoping to strike up a conversation with the woman in her fifties sitting next to me, I asked, "Where are we?" I expected her to respond with the name of the village or the city ahead. "We're getting close to the *Severny* [northern] checkpoint," she replied instead, pointing out the buildings in the distance. After a while, I asked her the same question once more. "We just passed the checkpoint at the entrance to Khasavyurt." I had a similar exchange later, in August 2012. As my marshrutka was nearing Makhachkala, I called a friend to tell her where I was. One of the passengers, a man in his fifties, overheard my conversation and chimed in: "Tell her we're crossing the checkpoint at the entrance to Makhachkala," even though the checkpoint had been dismantled long ago (the apparent reason why I had trouble determining my location).

The road was experienced as if divided into checkpoints and the stretches between them and measured in terms of distance to the nearest checkpoint.[20] Often, the very memory of a checkpoint or place in which a special operation had been carried out was a memory of violence, an immersion in the space of violence, which was then naturally normalized. Checkpoints, government buildings, private buildings guarded by masked men, policemen on patrol armed with rifles, administrative buildings surrounded by high fences, partly burned buildings (or the places in which they once stood) have become permanent fixtures of the Makhachkala landscape. The men who patrol the area in police jeeps, often sporting balaclavas or bulletproof vests, appear and disappear, and by doing so, they redefine the spaces of violence—areas that are best avoided, just as it is best to avoid "the state."

"My neighbor crosses the street whenever she sees a jeep. She's afraid it might explode," Gula, a forty-five-year-old accountant, told me over tea in her apartment in Makhachkala in October 2010. Over the previous summer, the city had witnessed an inordinately high number of bombings. "Marshrutka drivers give policemen and their cars a wide berth, too," she added.

The Magic of the State in Dagestan

"How naturally we entify and give life to such. Take the case of God, the economy, and the state, abstract entities we credit with Being, species of things awesome with life-force of their own, transcendent over mere mortals," Taussig writes in *The Magic of the State* (1997, 3). This "magic" makes itself known most emphatically in the periphery. In Dagestan, it is manifested through narratives

TORTURE, EXORCISMS, AND CHECKPOINTS   49

FIGURE 2.2.   Portrait of Vladimir Putin in a local kindergarten. Photo by Iwona Kaliszewska.

that present the state as an active causal agent and through "fantasies generated around the idea of the state" (Aretxaga 2003).

The following reflections concern instances in which my interviewees experienced the state, cases that depict the magical dimension of this entity in their lives.

Mariam's mother, Leila, mentioned earlier, spoke contemptuously of the local law enforcement agencies tasked with carrying out the fight against terrorism and despised the officers for resorting to violence when dealing with often-innocent people, their families, and their friends. Yet, Leila would frequently gaze adoringly into the television screen as she listened to Vladimir Putin speak, seeing in him a hope for a better future. She believed in the agency of his words and actions, including those undertaken as part of the fight against terrorism. It is in moments like these that the magical dimension of the state—a dimension that escapes deconstruction, even though there exist "rational" premises to do so—makes itself known. "Fantasy," Yael Navaro-Yashin (2002) writes, borrowing the term from Slavoj Žižek (1997), "survives deconstruction."

In Dagestan, fantasies about the notion of the state and the people who represent it draw on deep-seated imaginations, particularly ones regarding the state organisms of the former Soviet Union and imperial Russia. Additionally, the power of the state media creates a space in which state violence acquires other magical meanings, ones that remain powerful despite being abstracted from people's everyday lives. When discussed in the media, militants are almost invariably dehumanized; they are refused the right to a defense or trial, and their "elimination" is rationalized (see, e.g., Raubisko 2009). In my interviewees' narratives, the connection between Moscow's fight against terrorism and the violence employed against such people as Zumrut's husband was not apparent. The violence of the state at the level of local social practice—the tangible and familiar fight against terrorism witnessed on an everyday basis—was perceived, as I demonstrated earlier, to be unjust and a factor contributing to the deepening chaos and sense of danger. Meanwhile, many people rationalized the abstract violence that was supposedly directed at the "real" terrorists and saw it as justified. As Julia Eckert argues, "State violence is considered the right and duty of the state as much as it is a sign of its decay. It is abhorred and it is demanded. It is perceived as promising order and signalling chaos" (2005, 2). Below is an example of an account given by one of my interviewees, Jamilat, a woman in her early fifties, who mourns the relatives and neighbors killed in special operations.

> Stalin was able to exile all of Chechnya in two hours, send everyone to Kazakhstan or wherever. And yet they can't catch a couple of thugs? Whenever something explodes, they raid our homes and arrest innocent people. There used to be fewer cops and fewer problems, too. Isn't Russia the largest country on earth? What, am I supposed to believe they've run out of land? We work hard and they get money for nothing. But I'm sure that's how it works all over the world. . . . We need someone to rule with an iron fist, like in Stalin's time.

Thus, the dream of the distant, abstract power of a state that promises order coexists with the condemnation of the violence committed by local power structures. By calling for the elimination of terrorists, by promising "order" and publicly expressing his concern for the security of Russia's citizens, Putin becomes the guarantor of that security. The Russian media prominently employ the rhetoric of stability, which is often linked to the country's Soviet history, particularly to an idealized and simplified picture of the USSR that emphasizes security and a sense of confidence in the future. In Dagestan, the experience of the state fluctuates between a sense of danger evoked by the state's own security apparatus and the promise of security, stability, and the hope for justice. The "slippage between threat and guarantee" that Deborah Poole (2004, 36) writes about thoroughly permeates people's everyday lives. "I'm going to write a letter to Putin and let him know what's going on here! I just need to get his address. They already sent a letter to Moscow with pictures of the mansions our local government officials built for themselves, and they signed it: 'This is where your money goes.' Good. They ought to know about the outrageous things going on here," one of my interviewees, a man in his sixties, remarked angrily. Writing letters to the presidents of republics or to the Russian president himself is a well-established practice in the North Caucasus. The fact that these letters go unanswered is irrelevant. Ieva Raubisko writes about a Chechen man whose eighteen-year-old son was kidnapped by law enforcement officers, tortured, and imprisoned for one year. The father sought justice, writing letters to Chechen president Ramzan Kadyrov and Vladimir Putin in the belief that they would bring the perpetrators to justice. Despite all the suffering he had experienced at the hands of government officials, he honestly trusted that his leaders would take the path of justice and act fairly (Raubisko 2012). "He'd restore order if he wanted to! . . . He just doesn't know what's going on here! I'm sure he'd take care of it if he only knew. . . . Putin is our only hope. What we need is an iron fist," one of my interviewees said immediately after a televised speech by Putin, which he had listened to only in part.

This emotional attachment to the concept of a strong state—an abstract, omniscient agent acting on society—is so powerful that the idea itself resists deconstruction. It may even be described as an object of longing, in contrast to many of the practices carried out by local government officials, which are condemned and perceived as sources of violence and chaos.

Despite the complex social and political situation in the republic, Dagestan is rarely mentioned in the international media. Social researchers from Western countries hardly ever conduct studies in sociology, anthropology, or political science in Dagestan. The "struggle against international terrorism," as the Russian authorities attempt to frame the issue, is a peripheral conflict, one that is irrelevant in terms of geopolitics and media coverage. No international organizations are involved in its resolution, and the republic is rarely visited by Western journalists. Nor do many refugees from Dagestan arrive in Europe. Dagestanis who leave their homes—in fear of their own safety and for economic reasons—mainly migrate to the central and northern parts of the Russian Federation.

Although only a small fraction of Dagestani society is involved in the current conflict, it has nevertheless left a strong imprint in the daily lives of ordinary people: the fear of violence, arrests, and inspections at checkpoints has become internalized, engulfing both the body and the senses in a manner that is not always realized by the individual. The increasingly frequent and bold stories they heard of torture and persecution, paired with their own "encounters with the state," led my interviewees to perceive the state (which was manifested in the actions of the local authorities) as a source of unjustified, mindless violence that was further encouraged by local bureaucratic practices and rampant corruption.

The emotional attachment to the concept of an abstract and omnipresent state, powerful during the time of my research between 2019 and 2021, is beginning to fade.

Alexei Navalny's exposé of Putin's mansion in January 2021 and the COVID-19 pandemic have left Dagestanis disillusioned. Racked by political scandals and an economic crisis, the state has begun to lose its magic. The figure of Putin, which at the time of my research, inspired awe among various social classes, is slowly disintegrating. The president's public statements and promises are openly mocked on social media. Putin is no longer seen as a hero who will save Dagestanis from the army of corrupt officials but rather as a corrupt leader of his chiefdom. Even the evergreen narrative of unity and Great Patriotic War now fails to spark emotions. Is the eternal flame that was rekindled in 2005 dying out once again? We would have to ask the elderly Derbent resident who, in January 2021, roasted a shashlik over the eternal flame at the Great Patriotic War monument in the city's main square. A heated discussion ensued on Instagram: the culinary stunt outraged many of those who remained attached to this last mythical piece of "form," but an equally big number of posters (who have long since dispensed with such forms) defended the old man, arguing that it would make more sense to finally put the fire out and instead perform a *dua*, or prayer, for their veterans.

Is the Russian state losing its magic in the North Caucasus? Is it, to borrow Žižek's (1997) phrase, failing to "survive deconstruction" after all? The war in Ukraine will show.

CHAPTER 3

The Resurgent Importance of Islam in the Everyday Lives of Dagestanis

Religious and National "Revivals" in Dagestan

The growing importance of Islam in everyday life and politics was intertwined, in Dagestan, with the emergence of new power relations after the fall of the empire, particularly the processes of peripheralization (Derluguian 2005) and pauperization of North Caucasian societies. The "revivals" of Islam in the 1990s (and during the perestroika period) and in the first decade of the twenty-first century are connected but qualitatively distinct processes that occurred under different social and political circumstances. The first phase of the Islamic "revival" (for our purposes, approximately 1985–1999) coincided with a period of transition that accompanied the disintegration of the Soviet Union and saw the blossoming of various national "revival" movements. I have chosen 1999 as the caesura between the first and second phases, as it marks Vladimir Putin's ascendancy to power and the start of the Second Chechen War. Putin's centralization policies, along with the processes of peripheralization, the decline of ethnonationalist movements, and the transition to neoliberalism, resulted in the elimination of open political competition from the public sphere. This niche was subsequently filled by Islam, which came to be perceived as more than just "the faith of our ancestors" and became a way of life in its social and, increasingly, political dimension.

CHAPTER 3

FIGURE 3.1. Praying in a local mosque, Dakhadaevsky District. Photo by Iwona Kaliszewska.

I use the term *revival* to describe the increased presence and relevance of Islam in public life. I have chosen to place the word in quotation marks as it is not my intention to convey a romantic vision of a religion reawakened after seventy years of slumber. Other terms used in the literature include *Islamization* (Malashenko 2001) and, in reference to the processes occurring in the second phase, *shariatization* (Malashenko 2012). However, *Islamization* has established historical connotations and refers to the Islamization of Dagestan by Arabs in the seventh century, while the term *shariatization* clearly suggests the introduction of elements of sharia into public life, which has certainly taken place but is only one of several processes that make up a broader shift.

A Brief Historical Outline of the Islamization of Dagestan

Many accounts of Islam's revival in Dagestan following the collapse of the USSR open with descriptions of the Arab invasions in the seventh century (see, e.g., Malashenko 2001; Yarlykapov 2008; Yemelianova 2002). Although there is little continuity or direct causal relationship to be found between these processes, it is worth mentioning the events in the history of the Islamization of Dagestan that resurface in revival narratives, particularly in the first phase (the questionable role of historical narratives in the revival's second phase is discussed later in the chapter).

Islam arrived in the southern reaches of Dagestan with the Arab invasions of the seventh century and gradually spread north and westward (for further discussion, see, e.g., Shikhsaidov 1999). The raids were accompanied by the spread of culture, science, trade, and progressive northward Islamization. This process was a relatively slow one; until the sixteenth century, Islam coexisted in Dagestan with local religious practices as well as Christianity, which had been brought by missionaries from Caucasian Albania, Armenians, and Georgians. By the tenth century, the Arabs had Islamized the Lezgins, Rutuls, Tsakhurs, and Tabasarans, largely by force. By the end of the twelfth century, the faith had also been adopted by Laks and Aguls, then by the Dargins, Avars, Nogais, and Kumyks in the fourteenth and fifteenth centuries, and later by the Andis, the Tsez, and Akin-Chechens between the fourteenth and sixteenth centuries. In remote areas far removed from cultural centers, Islam coexisted with pre-Islamic faiths, and local *adats* (customary laws) superseded sharia. In the eighteenth and nineteenth centuries, Ghazi Muhammad, Gamzat-bek, and Imam Shamil waged war against the czar (Gammer 2002a; Zelkina 2000) while pursuing a campaign of shariatization, which they hoped would bring the highlanders under their rule. It was at this time that Sufism (a mystical and philosophical movement within Islam), particularly its Naqshbandi order, began to take root in Dagestan (see, e.g., Gammer 1994). Among the members of the order were all the future leaders of anti-czarist uprisings in Dagestan and Chechnya: Shaykh Mansur from the Chechen village of Aldi, and imams Ghazi Muhammad, Gamzat-bek, and Shamil. It is not entirely clear, however, what role Sufism played in the jihad against Russia (Derluguian 2001; Kemper 2002; Knysh 2007). The Russian conquest of the Caucasus was not synonymous with a fight against Islam or forced Christianization. Islam was seen as a cohesive factor that united the fragmented society of Dagestan; Russian authorities permitted sharia courts to operate, mosques and madrassas remained open (Yarlykapov 2000), and many Dagestanis traveled to Arab countries to study. The situation changed radically after the consolidation of Soviet rule (the Bolsheviks did not initially oppose sharia, nor did they interfere with the work of courts and mosques or the organization of local communities). The late 1920s witnessed the intensification of antireligious propaganda, accompanied by a campaign of repressions in which mullahs and qadis were targeted and mosques and religious schools were shuttered. Islam, as a religious practice, went underground. Sufi traditions and the practice of reading the Koran were continued, to a limited degree, in the home, among families, and in jamaats. A certain thaw occurred in 1941 when many Dagestani highlanders were recruited into the war effort, and authorities permitted some mosques to open. Up until the perestroika years, twenty-seven mosques legally operated in Dagestan under the supervision of the Spiritual Board of the Muslims of the North Caucasus, established in 1944 (Bobrovnikov, Muelfried, and Sokolovskiy 2011).

Islam's "eternal" presence on Dagestani soil, Imam Shamil's struggle against Russian colonization, and the fight to practice one's faith have all formed the bases of narratives and mythologies of revivalism, both among those who desire to revive old traditions, and among those who have mined history to find justifications for narratives that call for armed resistance against Russian rule. As a member of the Naqshbandi order, Imam Shamil became a hero to followers of Sufism, while his unbending resolve to spread the faith and his resistance to colonization made him a model for devotees of Salafism and all those who rejected religious divisions.

Does this rich repertoire of historical narratives, combined with notions and ideas rooted in the Soviet period, continue to influence Muslims' self-perception, their religious practices in the face of the social and political instability, and their attempts to find solutions to the conflict in the republic? I discuss these processes in greater detail in chapter 5.

Islamic Revival Processes, 1985–1999

The revival of Islam in the perestroika period and the early years of the Russian Federation mainly involved the increased presence of religious symbols in the public sphere. For a majority of the residents of Dagestan and Muslim regions of the USSR in general, the open expression of religious affiliation was something of a novelty. Soviet-era repression had pushed faith and religious practices into the private sphere, where it took on a strongly local character (Malashenko 2001, 64). Also local was the choice of signs and symbols used by individuals to identify themselves as Muslim (Omelchenko, Pilkington, and Sabirowa 2002). Knowledge acquired in the home was typically limited to elements of ritual, and Muslims were rarely familiar with the schools and branches of Islam or the details of religious practices.

The beginnings of the Islamic "revival" can be traced back to the period of liberalization ushered in by Mikhail Gorbachev in 1985–1991, manifested in such reforms as the 1990 law that permitted public displays of religion. In the North Caucasus, these years were marked by the construction of new mosques and the restoration of existing places of worship.

FIGURE 3.2. Restored mosque in Sivukh, Gumbetovsky Region. Photo by Iwona Kaliszewska.

Between 1985 and 1991, the number of mosques grew from 27 to 514. Four madrassas and forty-two maktabas (offering two- or three-year elementary Islamic education programs) were established in the same period, and 1,200 people made the pilgrimage to Mecca (Zalimkhanov and Khanbabayev 2000, 90). Islamic media and print journalism became increasingly important. A number of new periodicals began publication, including titles such as *As-Salam* (Peace), *Nurul-Islam* (The light of Islam), *Put' Islama* (The path of Islam), and *Islamskiy Vyestnik* (Muslim news). Islam was directly referenced in the programs of several newly established political parties, including Islamskaya Partiya Vozrozhdeniya (Islamic Renaissance Party), Jamaat ul-Muslimin (Muslim Community), Islamskaya Partiya Dagestana (Islamic Party of Dagestan), local chapters of the nationwide Nur (Light) movement, Soyuz Musulman Rossiyi (Muslim Union of Russia), and Muslimat, an organization for Muslim women. The Soviet-era Spiritual Board of the Muslims of the Caucasus split into seven separate boards, among them the Spiritual Board of the Muslims of Dagestan (DUMD). Sufi *shaykhs* began to appear in public life, along with a few Salafi leaders (Bagauddin Kebedov and Ahmad-Kadi Akhtaev, among others).

In analyzing the above data, which is highly typical for descriptions of religious revivals across the former USSR, it is important to bear in mind that many Dagestanis did not read Islamic newspapers, and that, at least initially, they visited mosques mainly out of curiosity; pilgrimages to Mecca were seen as a chance to travel abroad and sometimes as a business opportunity (Omelchenko, Pilkington, and Sabirowa 2002), while the activities of Islamic parties were limited to a narrow circle of supporters. Consequently, the above numbers provide little information about the scale of the resurgence of religious life (compare Rohoziński 2005, 130, in reference to Azerbaijan). In brief, the defining features of the religious attitudes of the time were highly eclectic rituals and views, growing interest in religious practices, "Muslim" names for newborns,[1] Islamic celebrations, and a reconsideration of the practice of alcohol consumption.[2]

Dagestan did not experience any significant religious divisions in the early 1990s. There were regional differences in terms of private religious practices, but the public expression of religious views (including prayers in mosques) was new to many Dagestanis, who learned about their faith from a variety of sources: the media, family members, and people who had received or were receiving a religious education. This knowledge varied significantly among individuals, regions, and education levels. With time, certain frictions emerged between efforts to revive local traditions and rituals, and the drive to standardize religious practices (Omelchenko, Pilkington, and Sabirowa 2002). For example, reading the Koran over the graves of the deceased—practiced in secret during the Soviet period—became all but socially compulsory and proved to be an awkward experience for many people who were unfamiliar with Islamic rituals and the proper recitation of prayers. Additionally, weddings and funerals were enormously expensive affairs and were beyond the means of some families during the crisis that followed the collapse of the USSR. Hence, the idea of reforming Islam fell on fertile soil. Still, the debates of the first half of the 1990s never went beyond disputes over the tenets of the Islamic faith and discussions about the essence of the religion.

What is striking in accounts of the national and religious revival are the significant parallels between both phenomena (compare Gammer 2002b). The intensity of the revivals is usually quantified in such terms as the number of periodicals and organizations, the presence of symbols in the public space (and ways in which they are deployed), and the number of people who identify with a given ethnic or religious category, though religious symbolism was sometimes included in national symbolism and would often become an integral element of it. Being a Muslim and participating in religious rituals became part of the national identity (compare Pelkmans 2011) and was also a means of socialization (Bobrovnikov, Muelfried, and Sokolovskiy 2011) but did not necessarily require a person to be religious. The boundary between ethnic and religious identity was a fluid one (compare Zapaśnik 2014, 44, in reference to Central Asia). The dynamics of national revivals appeared to dominate over public manifestations of religious life (compare Gammer 2002b).

National Revival Processes

Dagestan was the only republic in the USSR with such a large number of officially recognized ethnic groups. Soviet ethnographers formally recognized fourteen distinct ethnicities in the republic (the number of discernible ethnolinguistic groups is much greater). Each had its own newspaper, theater, and radio station. The Soviet Union also codified scripts for the languages spoken by individual ethnic groups. A Soviet citizen's ethnicity—listed in his or her "internal passport"—and ethnic heritage—cultivated at folklore festivals and in the names of regions (or republics, in other parts of the Soviet Union)—were important parts of the identities of the people inhabiting the various constituent entities of the Soviet Union. This was enormously significant at the time of its collapse.

Dagestan was also the only national republic within the Russian Soviet Federative Socialist Republic that was not established based on ethnicity. The name *Dagestan* simply means "land of mountains." The Avars, Tabasarans, Laks, Dargins, Lezgins, Rutuls, Kumyks, and Aguls are just some of the titular ethnic groups that inhabit the Republic of Dagestan. It can be said with only some exaggeration that these distinct ethnic groups were created during the Soviet period. They were constructed by Soviet social engineers and subsequently filled with content: codified writing systems, local folklore, theaters, and radio and television stations. Smaller groups, which were likewise recognized and classified by Soviet linguists and social engineers, were assigned to larger ones (e.g., the Didois, Andis, and Tindals were counted as Avars, while the Kubachins were counted as Dargins).[3]

The Soviet Union was the first modern state to have a federal system based in part on the criterion of nationality (Brubaker 1996). The USSR was intended to be a "free union of free nations," a federation of national Soviet republics. However, in the Soviet Union's formative period, there were no nations to speak of—not even in the sense attributed to the term by Soviet planners—in the North Caucasus, where social divisions followed the lines of clan or tukhum (federation) membership, rather than ethnic boundaries.

Dagestan existed as a separate republic from the beginning of the Soviet state. The "Mountain Republic," which comprised Dagestan and territory to its west, and was based on the community of highlanders and their shared

FIGURE 3.3. Women attend a religious holiday in Kubachi on June 22. Photo by Iwona Kaliszewska.

highlander identity, quickly disintegrated. It is unclear whether its collapse was precipitated by divide-and-conquer policies (history shows that the divisions that emerged in this period lay the foundation for later conflicts) or by the drive to carry out a great reform project and create an empire of free nations. These policies led to the creation of separate nations, defined as cohesive groups with their own distinct folklore. The development of Dagestani nations (ethnic groups) followed a similar path but was accompanied by the creation (or consolidation) of a trans-ethnic Dagestani identity and a sense of connection to the republic (Ware and Kisriev 2009, 28–31).

The 1920s and '30s saw the introduction of programs that were intended to encourage the development of Dagestani ethnic groups; more specifically, the ethnic categories created earlier were stocked with actual people. In Dagestan, however, there was little interest in the development of ethnic identities. National schools, newspapers, and theaters were established, and writing systems were standardized (initially based on the Latin script), but archival research shows that the reforms had little significance to the highlanders: neither the farmers nor the intelligentsia were particularly interested in developing distinct national cultures. According to official data, "the inhabitants of this society exhibited little consciousness of themselves as members of their officially recognized national groups." One possible reason for this is the fact that the inhabitants of the North Caucasus had much in common and shared a heritage that transcended ethnic and linguistic boundaries (Ware and Kisriev 2009, 28–32).

Dagestan was not spared the reification of nationality that defined the personal identities of Soviet citizens. With time, the ethnic categories by which the USSR classified its citizens—for example, by listing a person's ethnicity in his or her internal passport, or by promoting folklore—influenced Dagestanis, who began to strongly identify with their own ethnic groups while concurrently developing a Dagestani identity. In many ways, the Soviet federal system was, for them, a "big jamaat." Just as the jamaat was a polity broader than kinship structures, Dagestan and the entire USSR were political structures that transcended ethnic categories (Ware and Kisriev 2009, 32).

Reified ethnic distinctions resurfaced during the perestroika period, filling the void left by communist ideology in Dagestan to a much greater degree than religious ideas did. This phenomenon manifested itself in the formation of national movements by individual ethnic groups: the Avars, Lezgins, Kumyks, Laks, and Nogais. Members of these organizations lobbied for a narrow range of ethnic interests, demanding respect for the rights of their particular nation (the Kumyk national movement, for example, called for the expulsion of Avars, Dargins, and other highland nations from "historically Kumyk lands," while Akin-Chechens demanded the reestablishment of the Aukhovsky District, dissolved in 1944). The national "revival" gave youth and middle-aged people the opportunity to express their own ethnic identities, which had been both denied and emphasized under the Soviet Union (Brubaker 1996),[4] while offering them a chance to make a name for themselves in public life and to pursue self-realization.

It appeared as if Dagestan's ethnic diversity would become a source of instability (see, e.g., Ware and Kisriev 2009), but in fact the opposite happened. In Dagestan, conflicts that were initially interpreted and represented as ethnic strife were ultimately resolved without bloodshed (e.g., disagreements over land in the Novolaksky District, presented as a conflict pitting Chechens against Laks and Avars).

Dagestan's ethnic balance formed the basis for a political system unlike any other in the USSR in which all ethnic groups were proportionally represented in government. Put simply, the representatives in the Supreme Soviet of Dagestan were apportioned among the republic's many ethnic groups.[5] Despite the renewed institutionalization of ethnicity in post-Soviet Dagestan, ethnic divisions quickly transformed into rifts between individual jamaats. The heads of national movements lost interest in the concerns of the groups whose support they had mobilized and were soon revealed not to be leaders of individual ethnic groups, as had been hoped, but representatives of their own jamaats whose interests they pursued along with their own private aims. The political elite gradually became a jamaat of its own, in a process that was later entrenched by Putin's centralization policies, which reduced local politics to a demonstration of loyalty to the Kremlin.

Sooner than elsewhere in Russia, these actions engendered widespread disenchantment and indifference toward ethnic movements and possibly the question of ethnicity in general. Some leaders of ethnopolitical movements—the Khachilaev brothers, for example—were murdered for "too stridently" questioning the political status quo. Funding for national newspapers dried up, and their readers and staff drifted away. Mosques once associated with individual ethnic groups such as Avars, Kumyks, and Dargins gradually lost their ethnic character; sermons were given in Russian, the main language of communication among the congregation.[6] Islam became a unifying force that undermined particularism (Omelchenko, Pilkington, and Sabirowa 2002).

We may venture the claim that in general terms, the concept of ethnicity gradually returned to the status it held in the Soviet period. Although it continued to provide an interpretive frame in certain contexts, it played a diminishing role in everyday interactions, giving way to other increasingly popular interpretations and representations of reality, particularly religious ones, which were absent under the Soviet Union.

Islamic Revival Processes after 1999

The late 1990s and the beginning of the new century marked a clear turning point in Russia's domestic politics, particularly with regard to the Muslim Caucasus. As I explain below, these new policies had an enormous influence on political and religious divisions in the region and led to the emergence of an opposition between Sufism and Wahhabism.

The late 1990s witnessed the intensification of a conflict between two groups of Muslims: supporters and representatives of the DUMD and Sufi orders on the one hand, and Salafists on the other hand. The latter won support among young Dagestanis and intellectuals, who rejected the Islam practiced by Sufi orders as funereal, overly ritualized, and anachronistic. What began as a conflict over doctrine and the ritual aspect of religious practice turned into a political clash between the reformist camp and Dagestani authorities. The DUMD eventually succeeded in convincing the authorities that the reformists posed a threat not only to traditional Islam but also to Dagestan's political system and ruling elite. Yet, the Salafist movement was not initially perceived as a threat. Dagestani authorities tolerated, for example, the existence of a so-called Wahhabi enclave in the Kadar jamaat, comprising Karamakhi, Chabanmakhi, and a few other villages in the Buynaksky District, where in 1998 local Salafists drove out government officials and introduced sharia. In the eyes of the authorities, the main threats to the security and stability of the Caucasus were national movements and separatism, whose breeding ground lay in neighboring Chechnya, where Salafism was even less popular than in Dagestan. A significant shift in the perceptions of the reformist movement in Dagestan occurred in the fall of 1999, when radical Chechen and Dagestani Islamist forces invaded Dagestan.[7] This event convinced the authorities that Salafism—in both its militant and peaceful varieties—posed the greatest threat to the stability of the republic. The religious revival gradually acquired a new and increasingly political character (compare Gammer 2005).

In 1999, the government of the republic reached an unwritten agreement with the DUMD: from that point forward, the authorities would essentially support the board and call on Dagestani Muslims to be allegiant to it; in return, the DUMD would aid the government in the fight against Salafists. The DUMD and Sufi orders (particularly the murids of Shaykh Said Efendi) urged the authorities to rid the republic of Wahhabis once and for all. In response to these lobbying efforts, on September 19, 1999, the People's Assembly (the legislative body of Dagestan) passed a law titled "On the Prohibition of Wahhabite and Other Extremist Activity on the Territory of the Republic of Dagestan." Although it gave authorities significant latitude in determining who was or was not a Wahhabi and violated the constitution of the Russian Federation, which guarantees its citizens freedom of religion, the law was implemented by the government of Dagestan, where ignorance of laws and their willful violation were both commonplace.[8] The DUMD's Dagestani leaders subsequently adapted their rhetoric and actions to match the policies pursued by the Kremlin, which saw Wahhabism and other Islamic movements as proponents of Islamic extremism and international terrorism. The Sufism–Wahhabism dichotomy became strongly politicized. The authorities and the DUMD increasingly spoke about Wahhabism as a political activity synonymous with terrorism. There was a surge of anti-Wahhabism—that is, political rhetoric and actions directed not only against Salafists but against any movement or individual that challenged the existing power arrangement. Anti-Wahhabism thus provided a basis for collaboration between the secular political regime and the DUMD (Yemelianova 2002, 99). The authorities gained legitimacy and religious support, while the DUMD used this partnership to eliminate their ideological adversaries. It is not irrelevant that the amount of federal support received by the republic increased after 1999; according to data compiled by Bruce Ware and Enver Kisriev (2001, 106), federal funding grew by 270 percent. The influx of money benefited the government as well as the DUMD. Dagestani authorities launched what can be described as a witch hunt: reformers, even those who preached the use of peaceful means, became targets of a harsh crackdown, with many ending up in jail. Mosques believed to be Wahhabi places of worship were shuttered and their imams removed; Dagestanis were prevented from traveling to study in Islamic countries, where it was believed they would be infected by Wahhabi teachings. The dissemination of anti-Wahhabi propaganda was no longer limited to mosques and religious schools controlled by traditionalists: the authorities began actively supporting the DUMD by allowing the board to take over a large number of mosques, Islamic schools, and Muslim media outlets (including the largest Russian-language Islamic website, Islam.ru, and the newspaper *As-salam*). As the most powerful religious institution in Dagestan, the DUMD claimed a monopoly on overseeing matters involving Islam in the republic and assumed informal authority over all Dagestani Muslims. At the same time, media in the republic promoted the claim that the sole traditional (and permissible) stream of Islam in Dagestan was Sufism. Although there were forty to fifty Sufi orders active in Dagestan,[9] including twenty-three run by living shaykhs[10] (mainly the Naqshbandi and Shadhili tariqas), the DUMD only recognized four leaders of the Shadhili tariqa[11] as true shaykhs: Said Efendi Chirkeisky (murdered in 2012), Badrudin Botlikhsky, Arslanali Gamzatov (known as the Paraul shaykh), and Abdulvakhid Kakamakhinsky; the last three were subordinate to Shaykh Said Efendi (Pilkington and Yemelianova 2003). In result, the term *Sufism*, as used in the rhetoric of the DUMD, came to be associated with the religious practices of the Sufi orders sanctioned by the spiritual board and the authorities.

One consequence of these developments in Dagestan after 1999, particularly the persecution of Salafists, was the emergence of a hitherto barely existent militant underground.[12] The Salafists who supported armed conflict had emigrated to Chechnya in 1996, while peaceful Salafists worked publicly. Around 2004, Dagestani Salafists pledged allegiance to Chechen leaders and, with their support, launched a war against the authorities, security forces stationed in Dagestan, and representatives of the traditional stream of Islam. Forced underground, the Salafists had become radicalized. Whereas the Salafist movement of the 1990s was riven by internal divisions and encompassed a range of activists, from radicals like Ayub Astrakhansky to moderates who sought dialogue with the authorities (e.g., Akhmed-Kadji Akhtaev), after 1999 only the radical fringe remained politically and militarily active. Salafists who rejected military conflict receded from the political scene, concentrating instead on following the teachings of Islam in their daily lives, shunning labels, and often referring to themselves as "simply Muslims."

The armed Islamic underground played a much greater political role during my research than it did in the 1990s. The militants found support among many young Dagestanis, who referred to the fighters as "the jamaat"[13] and "the forest brothers." The idea of transforming Dagestan into an Islamic republic had recently entered the public discourse. The activation of the underground insurgency in 2009,[14] combined with the militants' effective online propaganda campaign and the influx of young members, sparked anxiety among Dagestan's political and intellectual elite, who fear the outbreak of a wide-scale armed conflict. Moscow's policy of ruling through violence, often implemented with the approval and support of local elites, has been a failure (Falkowski and Marszewski 2010). The witch hunt, kidnappings, and tortures only bolstered the ranks of the militants and their supporters, who often expressed approval for the extremists' ideas as a way of protesting the authorities' corruption. The militants' operations rarely targeted civilians but were instead directed against government officials, police officers, and members of the Ministry of Internal Affairs and Federal Security Service of the Russian Federation. With public confidence in the government waning and the perception of its actions as the primary cause of violence growing, these actions increased support for the militant insurgency in Dagestan.

CHAPTER 4

Wahhabis, Tariqatists, and "New Muslims"

Although calls for shariatization or an increase of presence of Islam in the public life were not rare, it was difficult to establish who was actually behind these calls and whether it was even a clearly identifiable group. Depictions of religious Muslims living in former Soviet republics usually employ a classification that casts them as either traditionalists or Wahhabis (or the axiological counterparts of these terms). Such labels as traditionalists and neotraditionalists are typically used to refer to members of Sufi orders and individuals who emphasize the importance of preserving traditional forms of religiosity. By contrast, adherents of reformist branches of Islam that strive to purify the faith of various local traditions are referred to as Wahhabis (or, with growing frequency, Salafis).

As I immersed myself in the world of Dagestani Muslims, I referred to the above categories as a framework of sorts, while understanding that they were a matter of convention. Assuming an anthropological perspective, I expected that although these categories would be fluid and subject to incessant shifts, they would nevertheless be relevant to the changes under way in the republic. Far from essentializing and attributing distinctive features to Wahhabis and traditionalists, I was interested in the social experience that came with belonging to Sufi orders and Salafi organizations. I was admittedly dismayed when, after a year of research, I had met *murids* (initiates) of the Dagestani shaykh Said Efendi (known as Chirkiesky after the name of his hometown) but had

WAHHABIS, TARIQATISTS, AND "NEW MUSLIMS"   67

failed to make contact with a single person who self-identified as a Wahhabi or Salafi. In time, I succeeded in tracking down self-declared Salafis, and Muslim clerics introduced me to the world of *madhhabs* (schools of law),[1] in particular to the Shafi'i school, the most popular madhhab in Dagestan. As I browsed internet forums, I happened upon discussions and debates between people who would classify their opponents as Wahs or Tariqatists, accusing each other of *shirk* (the worship someone other than Allah, for example shaykhs), practicing paganism, or extremism. I uncovered divisions. Most of my interviewees, meanwhile, would say about themselves, "We're Muslims—simply Muslims."

I initially believed that as I ventured deeper into the field and won the trust of my subjects, I would reach identities and divisions that remained hidden (mainly for reasons of security). I learned from Dagestani journalists that a large number of the mosques and religious schools in Makhachkala had a reputation for being either Wahhabi (*vakhovskiy, dzhamaatovskiy*) or Sufi (*tarikatskiy*,[2] *dumdovskiy*[3]). Yet, the religious map of the Dagestani capital also featured many mosques, schools, and madrassas that displayed no specific religious orientation. Among them was the local mosque in my neighborhood. My interviewees were people who had only recently turned to Islam and who based their knowledge of the faith on a variety of sources. They described themselves as "Muslims," "simply Muslims," or "new Muslims," downplaying the relevance of ethnic and religious divisions. I have chosen to use the term *new Muslims*, following the advice of Ekaterina Kapustina, who has conducted ethnographic fieldwork on migration in Dagestan and had also struggled to describe the religious affiliations of the people whom she interviewed. This was not the term I encountered most frequently in the field, but I have chosen to use it in order to emphasize my interviewees' relatively recent turn to Islam, a faith they experience and understand in different ways. A person describing him- or herself as a Muslim could be referring to a specific confession and their involvement in particular religious practices, but they could also be using the label as an ethnocultural designation for followers of Islam living in traditionally Muslim regions. Tatars, Bashkirs, Chechens, and other Muslims inhabiting the Russian Federation are described in the literature as "ethnic Muslims."[4]

"There's a war going on for those in the middle," Adallo, a man in his mid-seventies, told me in March 2009, when I asked him to tell me about new Muslims. Adallo was a Dagestani poet who had been under house arrest for supporting Wahhabism in the 1990s. He was of the opinion that "new Muslims would follow the strongest leader" and that they would have to decide where they stood. My interviewees did not strike me as undecided, but neither did they identify with any of the above categories. Some of them were careful to emphasize that they were "above all divisions" and downplayed the differences I sometimes hinted at in the phrasing of my questions. If we accept, after Gabriel Marranci and Daniel Martin Varisco, that it is not Islam that shapes Muslims but Muslims who shape and create Islam, then the religion that emerges from the practices of my interviewees is not Wahhabi Islam or Tariqatist Islam—each defined by differences in religious practice or their particular stance on Islamic law—but simply everyday Islam, a practiced and experienced faith in which these divisions play no prominent role. Being Muslim could have meant something different to each person, yet for all of my subjects, Islam was a type of framework: their knowledge of Islamic law and religious practices came from Friday sermons, discussions at the mosques, and the sermons by Islamic scholars that are widely available on the internet. Rather than write about the Islam of Tariqatists, Wahhabis, or new Muslims, I will focus on people's individual experiences as Muslims in Dagestan.

In a period of turbulent political shifts, the crisis of the state, and the strong politicization of Sufi and Wahhabi paradigms, it is crucial that descriptions of religious life in Dagestan account not just for the beliefs and experiences of individuals associated with Sufi orders, those who describe themselves as Salafis, and people involved in the peaceful Salafi religious movement Ahlu Sunna[5] but that they also examine the experiences of those in the middle—that is, people who have only recently turned to religion and whose faith is grounded in a variety of paradigms. My Muslims are not as much a group of faithful with distinctive features, united under a single organization with stated goals and a leader, as they are products of their time, firmly anchored in the local context and tightly bound to the peculiar nature of the religious and national revival[6] processes prompted by the dissolution of the Soviet Union, discussed in chapter 3. I begin with a discussion of the processes mentioned above, illustrating the manner in which the Sufi-Wahhabi dichotomy manifests in everyday life, while also reflecting on the mounting opposition to the actions of the authorities in Dagestan and the growing awareness of the goals shared by all Muslims. I then elaborate on the concept of new Muslims within this context.

The Sufi-Wahhabi Dichotomy

As a result of the political transformations described above, concepts such as Sufism, traditional Islam, Tariqatist Islam, Sufi Islam, and Tariqatism as well the terms *Wahhabism*, *Wahhabi Islam*, and *fundamentalism* have acquired a variety of meanings, ones associated with the politically charged sermons given by Muslim clerics and statements made by the authorities and state-controlled media. The Spiritual Board of Muslims of Dagestan (DUMD, see figure 4.1), with support from the government of the republic and the Russian Federation, began to advance a religious ideology that differentiated between "good" and "bad" forms of Islam: traditional Sufism (or traditional Islam) and nontraditional Wahhabism. Both of these labels were used in the media and in everyday speech to refer to a specific set of symbols: beards (or lack thereof), underwear, rolled-up pant legs, the practice of visiting *ustazes* and making the *ziyara*[7] (or the eschewing of such traditions), the celebration of Novruz Bayram (Spring Holiday), New Year, and the birth of the prophet (*Mawlid*[8]), as well as reading or avoiding literature classified by the DUMD as "extremist." The word *Sufism* (one of the elements of the dichotomy) therefore did not necessarily refer to the tradition of Islamic mysticism. The same was true of the term *traditional Islam*, which was not necessarily used only in reference to individualized religious practices steeped in local traditions. Both terms—*Sufism* and *traditional Islam*—encompassed the entirety of practices that were deemed acceptable by the DUMD and republic authorities and were not otherwise

FIGURE 4.1. Djuma mosque and Spiritual Board of the Muslims of Dagestan (*Muftiyat*) in Makhachkala. Photo by Iwona Kaliszewska.

classified as Wahhabism. By contrast, the terms *Wahhabism* and *Wahhabis* were used not in reference to the Islamic reformist movement guided by the belief that the Koran and the Sunnah are the sole basis for the faith, a movement inspired by the tradition passed down from the Hanbali theologian Muhammad ibn Abd al-Wahhab, but as a sort of epithet wielded by politicians and official media outlets in the former USSR to brand religious, political, and social organizations as well as individuals, much in the way anti-religious propaganda was deployed during the Soviet Union.

The Sufi-Wahhabi dichotomy and its attendant rhetoric on the part of the authorities and the DUMD was not without influence on everyday references and identities. Yet, its disconnection from everyday practices meant that this dichotomy gradually became subject to growing scrutiny, particularly after 2009. Over the course of several years of fieldwork, I encountered individuals who identified both with Sufi orders and Salafis. Certain religious practices that could be regarded as Wahhabi (based on the popular set of symbols) were clandestine and considered dangerous, while others were performed openly, displayed publicly, and regarded as safe. The boundary between beliefs and public practices was blurry; it was impossible to classify religious practices as either Sufi or Wahhabi. Moreover, where one stood in the dichotomy was often of little relevance in one's everyday life, everyday choices, and friendships, where it was more important to simply be Muslim and observe the teachings of the faith. Most people I met shared similar experiences with turning to Islam: there were many doubts, the least important of which were those pertaining to the ideological differences (or the DUMD's distinction) between Sufism and Wahhabism.

As I analyzed the field notes I collected between 2007 and 2009, I noticed that during that part of my fieldwork, I heard numerous stories of neighbors and distant relatives who had allegedly been brainwashed by Wahhabis. People shared advice on how to spot a Wahhabi: "the look in his eyes," "a beard and shaved moustache," "rolled-up pant legs," "no underwear," and in the case of women, "a black hijab or niqab" were all alleged signs. Anyone who completely gave up drinking or smoking was also immediately suspected of Wahhabism. Everyday habits or outfits that might have previously been regarded as innocuous became attributes that would draw the scrutiny of parents and relatives. I repeatedly heard different versions of the same narratives, questions, and concerns. "Is it curable?" "Is it a spell you can break?" worried one acquaintance whose son had simply begun praying and attending prayers at the mosque. "How can I tell if my sons have fallen into the clutches of Wahhabism?" (female, thirty-five years old).

In Dagestan, weddings and funerals are social spaces that bring together members of a tukhum (lineage), residents of a village, neighbors, colleagues, and classmates. Women and men are seated separately, questions are asked over tables filled with food—questions that very often spark emotional discussions about the wedding itself, about family members, and their often-complicated life trajectories. Between 2007 and 2012 a wedding with music and dances, and an abundance of food and alcohol, was considered (by most of my interviewees, especially the middle aged and elderly) to be a "proper" celebration (see figure 4.3), in contrast to a quiet wedding with nasheeds and no alcohol. It signified that the newlyweds and their family were not "affected by Wahhabism" and came as a relief to relatives, who often barely knew the young couple getting married, let alone their views on religion.

Comments were shared, over food and in hushed tones, about the absence of certain family members who refused to participate in the wedding (refusals to participate in funerals "for no reason" were less frequent); families who had allowed their loved ones to become Wahhabis were judged or pitied. "How could they have allowed it? Such a respectable family. . . . They must have lost control of them or overlooked the signs." "What did they do wrong? Maybe he will get over it soon." "What a tragedy [*takoe gorye*] for the whole family!" Some families cut ties with their loved ones for "joining the Wahhabis" and "turning their backs on their relatives." There was a general perception that Wahhabis were evil and foreign to Dagestani culture. Such statements were usually expressed amid general comments about the unstable situation in the

FIGURE 4.2. Wedding preparations, Kayakent District. Photo by Iwona Kaliszewska.

72 CHAPTER 4

FIGURE 4.3. Traditional Dargi wedding in Makhachkala. Photo by Iwona Kaliszewska.

republic, for which Wahhabis were to blame. "Every last Wahhabi needs to be killed in order to keep the peace!" said one elderly man. There were references to Stalin, who "would have known what to do with them long ago" (male, fifty-five years old). He felt threatened not only by the Wahhabis but by a general rise in piety (which was often seen as a suspicious sign that a person was on his way to becoming a Wahhabi). Narratives and emotional statements like the ones above were not rare and very often were expressed in response to general complaints about the realities of post-Soviet life and living standards in the North Caucasus. Sometimes they were a direct result of the DUMD's teachings, in which Wahhabism was portrayed as alien to Islam. The DUMD's potential to present their teachings (including their stance on Salafi-oriented Muslims) as compliant with the normative discourses is also an important factor to consider.

"It's best to stay away from Wahhabis. Don't make friends with them—they're dangerous," said Magomed. He was 22 years old and lived with his parents, unable to find a job. He hung out with a group of peers his age or younger. It is from them that he "acquired" Islam. His parents were of a middle-class first generation rural-urban migrants, not religious, a bit nostalgic towards the USSR and relatively successful in the market economy. They were concerned about Magomed becoming observant and being unemployed. They feared he would be attracted by the Wahhabis, so they provided him with videos and books on the "Wahhabi threat" issued or approved by the DUMD.

"They're not Muslims—they're thugs!" he continued. "They give Islam a bad name. They ought to get rid of every last one of them! I'm sure they're getting paid in dollars. Why else would anyone join them?"

"Who's paying them?" I asked.

"Forces that are bent on destroying Russia. Organizations from England. I saw a show about it on TV. They're getting paid. Why would anyone join them? They're brainwashed. I can give you a copy of the DVD *The True Face of Wahhabism*, and you'll see what Wahhabism is all about. It explains everything. Do you have a USB drive?" Magomed put various anti-Wahhabi films on my pen-drive, films that were widely accessible in some of the Islamic shops and on internet sites.

Only later did I discover that Magomed and his friends, who embraced what I considered to be a black-and-white stance on "Wahhabism," knew some young men in their city who were considered to be "Wahhabis." "Look, the Wahhabis live over there!" said the oldest in the group, pointing to a blue gate on the main street in Kyzylyurt, as we were driving towards a mosque. "Are you scared?" joked Magomed. "No worries, these are our Wahhabis; they're peaceful Wahhabis," continued the oldest.

On our way back to Magomed's apartment, his friend drew my attention to a half-burned house. "They [armed forces, police] bombed [*bombili*] that place for twelve hours last month and killed one person. It's understandable. They get paid by the hour." The young men did not know the people who lived in the house, but knew their relatives, from whom they had heard that the inhabitants were "accused of Wahhabism."

The speeches, sermons, and publications of the DUMD, echoed in turn by state officials, were successful (at least between 2005 and 2009) in creating and maintaining a moral panic around Wahhabism. There was, however, a distinction between the elusive foreign Wahhabis portrayed by the media and "our Wahhabis," who somehow did not fit the picture. It is important to note, however, that the support for the annihilation of Wahhabis did not necessitate support for the military actions carried out by local and federal authorities, especially when these took place in a person's own neighborhood. Army and police operations were often perceived as money laundering and rackets set up to extract bribes from the local community, whose members were appalled by such campaigns. They believed that the *siloviki*[9] would often knock down the wrong doors. As the number of special operations grew, so did the doubts about the people they were targeting, especially if they were relatives or neighbors.

Although some of my friends continued to share stories about young people who had been brainwashed by the Wahhabis, more and more people were beginning to doubt the veracity of these tales. "Has anyone even seen these Wahhabis?" (man, approximately thirty years old). "Are they even real?" "This all sounds strangely convenient for someone." "They made up Wahhabis so they'd have someone to blame for their problems." "*They're* the real Wahhabis [the authorities, the siloviki]" (woman, approximately thirty years old). The narrative shifted in 2009–2010. Instead of stories about "wicked devils," I would hear reports about an atheist who had been "turned into a Wahhabi" by the siloviki, who had killed him after he had come out of his house brandishing a weapon, yelling "Allah akbar!" and how Wahhabism was being used as a cudgel against political opponents (man, approximately sixty years old). The same subjects who had grumbled about Wahhabis just one year earlier were now growing increasingly skeptical of their supposed responsibility for the rampant corruption and the crisis of the state. "There's nothing wrong with Wahhabism itself. Wahhabis are Muslims just like us. Wahhabism is the official religion of Saudi Arabia and look how well they're doing" (woman, fifty years old). I also encountered the terms *peaceful Wahhabi* and *peaceful Salafi*, used to emphasize the nonviolent nature of these communities and to distinguish them from militants who resorted to violence.

By 2010 and 2011, my questions about Wahhabis began to elicit different responses: "One of my friends is a . . . well, you know . . . what do call them . . . a Wahhabi, and he's a decent guy" (man, thirty-four years old); "My daughter's husband, he's a . . . he doesn't go to weddings, he doesn't drink—any girl would be lucky to have a husband like him!" (woman, fifty years old); "They call them Wahhabis. Let me tell you, if everyone was like those Wahhabis and lived their lives that way, then the world would be a better place" (woman, approximately fifty years old).

The word *Wahhabi* gradually disappeared from the everyday vocabulary of Dagestanis. The aggressive, heavily funded—and ostensibly successful—propaganda campaign by the DUMD did not produce the expected results. The anti-Wahhabi rhetoric seemed to have taken root only superficially: Wahhabis were decried in certain contexts, "appropriate" printed matter was displayed conspicuously, and accusatory speeches were made in the presence of larger (or untrusted) groups. Certain analogies (albeit possibly superficial ones) can be drawn to the mindless repetition of Soviet rituals such as May Day parades, speeches, and assemblies, which existed as a form that was increasingly removed from social practices and actions.

The DUMD achieved greater, more lasting, and most importantly, more tangible results through its campaign to increase the public presence of Islam via such outlets as the website Islam.ru and the newspaper *Assalam*, both of which are associated with the board. Efforts such as lobbying for the introduction of classes on the fundamentals of religion in the Dagestani public school curriculum, the establishment of an Islamic education system, the support for limits on the sale of alcohol, the banning of gambling, aiding the fight against prostitution, and calls for the legalization of polygamy all met with a positive response. Crucially, the public supported specific measures rather than the DUMD in general. Social campaigns carried out by the DUMD and grassroots efforts by particular communities and their respected members (regardless of where they stood on the matter of Salafism versus Sufism) increased the presence of Islam in the public sphere and in the minds of Dagestanis.

By the late 2000s, Islam had gone from being a "feature of the national identity" to a way of life, and a growing number of mosques and madrassas were being built. With each passing year, it became increasingly rare to see men smoking in the streets of Makhachkala (women who smoked did so in the privacy of their own homes even before this period). Women could be seen wearing the hijab, and growing numbers of people attended daily prayers at mosques. In the month of Ramadan, many restaurants and cafés would close during the day, and in 2011 and 2012 numerous stores posted signs stating, "No alcohol for sale" (possibly prompted not by religious principles but by fear of the gangs that were going around collecting money for jihad from infidels). More and more marshrutka drivers were playing nasheeds[10] and Islamic sermons in their vehicles instead of the traditional Russian or Dagestani pop songs. It was difficult to order a taxi during afternoon prayers on Friday. "Sorry, there are no drivers available right now. Everyone's at *ruzman* [the main Friday prayer service]," one cab dispatcher told me. Questions such as "Are you a believer?" and "Do you pray?" became ritual questions posed to newly met people. As late as 2005, the list of standard questions included inquiries about a person's national identity. Vladimir Bobrovnikov points out that overt manifestations of Islamization in Dagestan were not accompanied by commensurate increases in religious knowledge. In his view, low academic standards at universities, madrassas, and maktabs, paired with the superficial knowledge of Islam prevalent among contemporary Muslim scholars are evidence against a supposed "spiritual revival of Islam." Bobrovnikov provides convincing data and examples; however, based on my own observations in the field, I am inclined to believe that this twenty-first century religious revival has simply assumed a different form, one that corresponds to the present social and political transformations. An increasing number of people described themselves as "simply Muslims," defining themselves not in terms of their social or ethnic group but by stating their religious affiliation, one that did not necessarily fit into the Sufi-Wahhabi dichotomy.

Simply Muslims, Muslims, and New Muslims

The Sufi-Wahhabi dichotomy left a strong mark on the political landscape of Dagestan in the first decade of the twenty-first century. The categories of good and bad Muslims, traditional and nontraditional Islam, and safe and unsafe Islam were constantly present in political rhetoric. I was initially convinced that these divisions were being hidden from me and that statements such as "There is only one Islam and we are all Muslims" were intended to show me that the speaker's version is the right one or even to imply that there was no point in talking to people who understood or practiced Islam differently. It seemed important to apply these sorts of categories in my fieldwork so that I could describe the social reality of my subjects. However, I eventually understood that my interviewees were not denying the existence of this categorization—they were simply refusing to be placed in it.

Many people attempted to place themselves in the category of traditional Islam when speaking to me for the first time, emphasizing their distinctness from Wahhabis (whom they described using the distinguishing features mentioned above). These individuals typically did not challenge the statements and practices of shaykhs directly, which does not necessarily mean that they identified with Sufism. In light of the rampant persecution and the growing awareness that anyone, even a nonbeliever, could be branded a Wahhabi, this attitude seemed to be a safer strategy. "In the complicated web of discourses from which emerge various 'distinctive' features of religious identity, individuals are never entirely free in their choices," writes the Latvian anthropologist Ieva Raubisko, describing the religious beliefs of Chechen Muslims. "Rather, they are bound in a never-ending process of negotiating between their own developing (or developed) convictions and the ideas that are considered to be the beliefs of the majority" (Raubisko 2009, 88). The boundary between the practiced and the believed, between the concealed and the revealed (particularly to outsiders) is blurred and shifts depending on the context, the interlocutor, and his or her trustworthiness.

My awareness of the tentative nature of Sufism and Wahhabism as categories did not prevent me, at least not initially, from classifying the religious beliefs and practices of people whom I encountered for my own purposes. Although I realized the pointlessness of such classifications, I was not immediately able to escape this dominating frame of thought. As I reanalyze these interviews, I understand in retrospect that my questions prompted my interviewees to place themselves in, or cut themselves off from, one of these categories. Whenever I attempted to classify someone, I would be told to approach a "real" murid or Wahhabi. In March 2009, after Friday prayers, an acquaintance—a man in his late twenties—and another man entered a store in which I had been sitting for several hours. Laughing, the acquaintance introduced us. "This is our Wahhabi," he said. "She wanted to meet a Wahhabi," he explained to the somewhat embarrassed man. "Ask him whatever you want," he added. The man likely felt as awkward about the situation as I did, especially since shoppers were now filing in after Friday prayers. As a consequence of this experience, I became more careful about the questions I asked and more able to deconstruct in my head the Sufi-Wahhabi dichotomy that loomed over my research and my perception of the reality I was studying.

The more I learned about my subjects and the more time I spent with them—talking, drinking tea, listening to Muslim preachers, nasheeds (Islamic hymns), and hits from *Fabrika Zvyozd*[11]—the more it became apparent to me that I would have to transcend the Sufi-Wahhabi dichotomy in describing their world and their lives.

In 2007–2011, during the phase of my research in which I focused most heavily on religious practice, I observed a marked increase in my subjects' interest in learning about Islam. The nature and content of our conversations was also changing, as was my (and my interviewees') knowledge of religious practices. Nearly everyone I talked to admitted that the primary influence in their turn toward religion had been another person whom they considered wiser and more knowledgeable on the subject of Islam. This was not always an older person: often a peer, colleague, relative, or neighbor would talk to them about Islam or lend them a DVD or book on the fundamentals of the faith, the story of the Prophet Muhammad, or the history of the first four caliphs. Other popular reading material covered the technical aspects of prayer, the positioning of the body during the namaz, and the duties of Muslim men and women. My interviewees were much more eager to read books and watch DVDs about the tenets of the faith than the fiery, hostile sermons by the DUMD ideologues waging war against Wahhabism. Islamic stores in my neighborhood carried increasingly large stocks of religious book and guides, translated from Arabic, with titles such as *How to Pray Namaz*, *How to Be a Good Wife*, and *Islamic Medicine*. There were also Russian-language versions of DVDs titled *Understanding Allah through Reason* and *Koranic Miracles*—the evidence for the existence of Allah provided in these films often cropped up in my conversations. The most popular among them was the story of a sheep whose wool had apparently arranged itself to form the word *Allah*: I would often spot a photograph of this animal on my subjects' smartphones. As I explored the field, I learned that some of the stores I frequented were seen as either Wahhabi or Sufi. Hoping to provoke conversations in Wahhabi stores, I asked about books on Dagestani shaykhs, recordings of their public statements, and so forth. I would be told politely that they did not carry such items but that the store next door might. Most of the salespeople whom I encountered for the first time treated me as a local woman interested in learning more about Islam. I was not always forthcoming with the purpose of my research or the fact that I was not from Dagestan, as I was curious to see where the conversation would lead. If the staff of a store were aware of the purpose of my visit, they would tell me about Russians who had converted to Islam and encourage me to learn more about the religion.

Whether I introduced myself as a Polish academic who was interested in Islam or just browsed the books and recordings and chatted with the salespeople, religious bookstore staff would invariably treat me as "spiritually curious." I would often be given recordings of lectures and sometimes miswak sticks or imported Arab cosmetics. I would never receive explicitly Sufi or Wahhabi material unless I specifically asked for it. Nor would salespeople recommend any of the easily available records and books containing anti-Wahhabi propaganda. Such publications were often laid out in plain view, even in Islamic clothing stores that did not stock literature or audio recordings. As the clerk in one store, a woman in her mid-thirties, explained, "Some people, especially the police, have trouble understanding that we don't sell anything illicit here. They see a girl like me wearing the hijab and they call me a 'Wahhabi,' a terrorist. That's why we lay these books out—just to be on the safe side," she said, gesturing at a pamphlet titled "Warning: Extremism!" displayed on her desk.

After spending many hours in Islamic stores talking to the salespeople and customers, I realized that many, perhaps even most, of these individuals could be described as "spiritually curious" and knew little about religion. They would stop by these stores to purchase cosmetics, recently popular Islamic medicine, black cumin oil, amulets for drivers, Mecca calendars, prayer beads, and rearview mirror surah pendants. As I talked to them, I realized that they had little grasp of the ideological differences between Wahhabis and traditionalists and that these divisions were of little relevance to them.

Mariam

Mariam, aged thirty, was a regular customer of a store in my neighborhood of Makhachkala. She began visiting the establishment due to its proximity to her marshrutka stop but remained a loyal patron because of the people whom she would meet at the store, particularly Rizvan. Mariam came from a family in which religion did not play a significant role. Her parents were engineers who had grown up in the city. I had known Mariam since 2005, but it was only in 2009 that religion became a topic of discussion among members of her household. Surahs from the Koran, pictures of Mecca, and Islamic calendars appeared on the walls of their home. My hosts were not able to translate the surahs, but they emphasized the beauty of the inscriptions. They seemed to have been strongly influenced by recently converted friends and relatives, who used social gatherings as opportunities to share the changes they had experienced in their lives and the help they had received from Allah. These were not theological discussions but simply everyday conversations during which advice would occasionally be shared. Sometimes they would leave a newspaper; other times they would offer the family a book. Influenced by these encounters, the family members made Islam an increasingly important part of their lives; Mariam's father would browse *Assalam* between the news and the variety shows on TV. Mariam would fall asleep to the sound of nasheeds wafting from her stereo. Her mother would occupy her free time with a radio program about the benefits of preparing meals according to Islamic principles. Every morning, she and Mariam would each swallow a teaspoon of black cumin oil from the Islamic store. In their bathroom, there were now miswak sticks and toothpaste from the same shop, which Mariam visited once or twice a month. The shopkeeper and his friend Rizvan encouraged the girl to pray and participate in religious practices. The store had a reputation as a Wahhabi establishment—a fact that Mariam learned from me but that was also of little concern to her. In contrast to Huseyn and Magomed, whose stories I present below, she was uninterested in politics and was unaware of the politicization of religious identities and would draw on symbols regarded as Wahhabi and Sufi more or less at random.

Huseyn and Magomed

I met Huseyn, aged thirty-eight, in the spring of 2008. He appeared to be rather wary of my colleague[12] and me during our first conversation. He talked about

Tsumada, his home region, and about tradition and Islam. He mentioned that he had a shaykh in his family (leading me to conclude that he was not a Wahhabi) but did not explore this topic further. When we met again two years later, he spoke with much greater candor about himself and his dilemmas.

"Who am I, really? One of my ancestors was a shaykh, a respected, upstanding person. Yet, I don't make the ziyara, I don't visit shaykhs, and I'm not a murid. But I do take part in the *dhikr* at a funeral, as you saw. How could I not pay my respects to the dead? I couldn't do that to his family," he added, referring to the funeral we had attended the previous day, for a policeman killed in a special operation.

"But if you look at my beliefs, then I'd say I'm closer to . . . you know . . . Wahhabis. They're right: there's no need for intermediaries or all the superfluous rituals that grew out of tradition. Islam in its pure form is fine for me."

"There are many others like me," he continued, trying to answer my question about the words *Sufism* and *Wahhabism* and their common use in the media.

Huseyn realized that people who did not subordinate their practices to the DUMD were treated unjustly. He condemned the security services for treating innocent, devout Muslims as militants and said he understood why radical ideas were gaining traction in Dagestan.

"They have no choice. There's a limit to how much abuse and humiliation they can endure," he said.

"The call us all Wahhabis. If you roll up your pant legs, you're a Wahhabi. If you wear a beard, you're a Wahhabi. . . . I wish I could grow a beard like the Prophet Muhammad, but people wouldn't understand, especially in my family's village. Our imam is very strict about these things: no exceptions."

"What good are all these divisions in Islam? We're all Muslims," he said.

Huseyn did not feel the need to "define himself," to take a stand on either side. What mattered most to him was regular prayer, following the rules of Islam, and setting an example for others so that they, too, would accept Islam and pray.

Magomed, aged thirty-four, faced similar dilemmas. I met him in 2009 in a mountain village in the Tsumada region. He was not a member of any order: "That's something they do down there, on the plains," he said. He would visit graves on the Muslim holiday marking the end of the month of fasting (Ramadan Bayram or Eid al-Fitr) and take part in the prayers held at the cemetery (see figure 4.4). "There are people in our village who don't go to the cemetery. They say that the Koran forbids it. It depends on who you ask. Maybe they're right. But it's also important to honor the memory of your ancestors. . . . I don't know what to think."

WAHHABIS, TARIQATISTS, AND "NEW MUSLIMS" 81

FIGURE 4.4. View of the cemetery in Kvanada, Tsumadinsky Region. Photo by Iwona Kaliszewska.

When we met again the next year, Magomed had been listening to the sermons of Said Buryatsky (recommended, he told me, by a friend who "knew a lot about Islam"), considered to be one of the leading ideologues of the Caucasian jihad movement. The recording caused Magomed to run afoul of a local FSB officer. "I'll listen to whatever I want," he said without switching off the sermon. "It's a wise sermon, by the way," he added. Our conversations gradually shifted from differences in religious practices (which I emphasized and picked up on) to the subject of violence. Magomed was increasingly concerned about the situation in the republic and about the ongoing persecution of innocent people. I learned from other sources that Magomed's cousin had been killed by security forces in a special operation—likely the same one that took the life of the policeman whose funeral I had attended a few days earlier.

There were many people like Huseyn and Magomed among the subjects I interviewed. They were conscious of the discursive distinction between Wahhabis and Tariqatists but would base their own beliefs and practices on many sources: personal encounters with other Muslims, conversations they had in mosques, visits to Islamic stores and local healers, and DVDs. My observation and analysis of their methods of learning about Islam led me to the conclusion that my subjects could not be said to draw on content labeled "Wahhabi" or "Sufi" by the DUMD; rather, they transcended these distinctions entirely.

New Muslims?

I met many people like Huseyn, Magomed, and Mariam over the course of my research. Among them was Jamilat, who often repeated how important Islam was in her life and how it influenced her behavior. She regretted that her husband, who was unfaithful to her, was not devout: she longed for his return to Islam and become a pious Muslim. There was also Shamil, who had studied in Iran and was as eager to convert me to Islam as he was to take me out to dinner. Our conversations about Islamic virtues were interspersed with stories of the women he had met at student parties in Tehran, and the hijab-wearing girls who had invited him over to their homes in supposed attempts to seduce him.

Each of these individuals had only recently turned to Islam. They followed similar paths in their daily exploration of their faith: conversations with friends and relatives, attending the mosque, trips to Islamic stores, reading books, and watching DVDs. Like Mariam, they initially treated Islam as the object of their spiritual curiosity, and like Huseyn, Magomed, and Jamilat, many later came to see it as a way of life, a crucial and indispensable part of their being. As I became acquainted with my subjects, our superficial, preliminary conversations led to debates on the nature of God, the differences between Christianity and Islam, and talks about life, death, and violence. Many of my interviewees simply wanted to share with me their fervent beliefs and to underscore the central role of Islam in their lives, regardless of the sources from which their knowledge of the religion came. Discursive divisions remained separate, as if outside the realm of their religious practices, everyday choices, and their identities. The concurrent ubiquity and absence of this dichotomy prompted me to focus my attention on Muslims and simply Muslims—individuals whom I refer to as new Muslims as a way of emphasizing their recent turn to religion and in order to differentiate them from ethnic Muslims, or people who had been raised in the Muslim faith, who often described themselves as Muslims but in whose lives religion did not play a significant role.

I have encountered the term *new Muslims* used in reference to the North Caucasus on several occasions. Anna Matveeva and Igor Savin (2012), authors of the report *North Caucasus: Views from Within*, also mention new Muslims (alongside Tariqatists and Wahhabis), whom they describe as peaceful Salafis (*mirniye salafity*). This understanding of the term differs from my usage, but the very fact that the authors have transcended the Sufi-Wahhabi dichotomy typically encountered in analytical texts strikes me as noteworthy. The concept of new Muslims is also employed by Irina Babich and Akhmet Yarlikapov (2003) in reference to Muslims in Kabardino-Balkaria. The faithful in question were associated with the Islamic Center, founded in 1993 and renamed the Institute of Islamic Research in Kabardino-Balkaria in 1999. The new Islam represented by this group cannot be identified with either the Wahhabi school or "traditional Islam," which its members opposed. Their main goal was to protest the authorities' interference in religious matters and to speak out against the persecution of religious people and anyone who was dissatisfied with the actions of the government. The founders of the movement—Ruslan Nakhushev, Anzor Astemirov, and Musa Mukozhev—and its members did not intend to resort to violence: in 1999, they denounced Shamil Basayev's call for violent insurrection and were careful to avoid outside influence and funding, fearing that missionaries from Arab countries would impose their own foreign interpretation of Islam locally. Yet, these new Muslims in Kabardino-Balkaria were disregarded by the authorities. Facing mounting persecution, they unwillingly withdrew into the margins of the political realm, into the underground. Within a few years, they were essentially forced to collaborate with Basayev, leading to the violent 2005 uprising in Nalchik, the capital of Kabardino-Balkaria, in which 134 people were killed and many were injured. Although the social and political circumstances in the two republics are too different to permit extensive comparisons between their respective Muslims populations, the two communities undoubtedly share experiences of violence and the crisis of the state and are united in their opposition to persecution, torture, and other methods practiced by the authorities. Muslims in Kabardino-Balkaria mounted an organized effort to influence the authorities of the republic. Their Dagestani counterparts, by contrast, increasingly withdrew from the state and gradually ceased to "speak the same language"; although they formed communities in cities and mountain auls, they established no organization that would lobby for change in the republic at the local or regional level. By remaining outside the system of political divisions, they form an overlooked grassroots force, one that could potentially play a key role in a future large-scale conflict.

CHAPTER 5

Sharia

Thinking beyond the (Secular) State?

The way in which Dagestanis think about nonviolent coexistence beyond the state hews surprisingly close to Walter Benjamin's ideas about the state's presence and absence in the everyday, formulated nearly a century ago. Let me begin this chapter with a short excerpt from an interview with James Martel about Benjamin's (1996, 1:236–52) "Critique of Violence":

> What Benjamin shows us, I think, is not only that a nonviolent life is possible, but that it exists all around us. We are actually engaged in it already. In his view, nonviolence is just another name for daily life, for the infinite decisions, agreements, arguments, and resolutions that we all make with one another each and every day and without any recourse to law or the state. This is what I like to call the anarchist life that we are already living. Nonviolence, then, is not some pie-in-the-sky utopia but an ongoing presence that we always have recourse too. We do not need to destroy everything and then start over. Rather we must remove the parasitic and mythic overlord that rules us through its violence and its lies. The greatest deception that mythic violence has ever pulled over on us is the notion (popularized by novels like *Lord of the Flies*) that if the state or other archist forms were to remove themselves from our life, we would all be stabbing one another within minutes. Benjamin shows us that it is the state itself, the veritable fox guarding the henhouse, that is

the source of violence in our life. We may respond to it with various acts of violence of our own, but that is only to repeat the way that we are enmeshed in a violent and mythic order. (Evans 2020)

In Dagestan, dreams of nonviolent coexistence surfaced frequently in conversations with my subjects, but few of them actually expected the state to guarantee it. Rather, they expected the state not to interfere in their lives or even to withdraw from their lives entirely. The path by which order would be achieved was set out not by the state officials but by imams, leaders of religious communities, Muslim healers, and other authority figures. One community might pursue order through temperance, another might emphasize a "traditional" upbringing, and yet another may impose order through the equivalent of a Soviet kolkhoz, now run as a private enterprise. The growing relevance of Islam in the republic means that this "multiplicity of orders" which, according to Jean and John Comaroff (2008), defines the social realities of postcolonial countries—many features of which are common to Dagestan—gradually coalesced into a single order founded on various forms of sharia.

Many of the people I talked to followed the rules of sharia in their daily lives, convinced that the popular shariatization of society would bring about the order that the state failed to provide. Such practices as the namaz performed five times daily, fasting during the month of Ramadan, and the pilgrimage to Mecca were become increasingly present in their lives. "New Muslims" spread knowledge about Islam and the Islamic way of life that would "heal the republic and prevent its collapse." They longed for order for themselves, their communities, and Dagestan. Some of them believed that no change was possible without the practical implementation of an Islamic state, which was increasingly becoming a topic of open discussion in the republic.

As I heard the ideas and visions of change preached by Dagestani Muslims, replete with references to past events and experiences on which the future was to be modeled, I was shocked by their uncompromising slogans: "Only sharia will save Dagestan," "Only in an Islamic state will there be justice," "We want to live according to Islamic law," "We don't want to live in a state run by unbelievers and hypocrites [*kafiri* and *munafiki*]." Because these statements were supported with numerous quotations from the Koran and were delivered with visible emotion and conviction, I initially interpreted them as manifestations of resistance or even radicalism. These convictions were reaffirmed by people from "secular Makhachkala" with whom I shared and discussed my observations.

Whatever the original subject of our conversation was, most of my subjects in religious Makhachkala steered the discussion toward Islam, the situation in the republic, the need for change, and the efforts that were being undertaken to achieve it. They spoke of the blessing that Islam would bestow on people, nations, and the entire world. I visited villages in which sharia had been imposed, I listened to people talk about Islamic law and the Islamic vision of the state, and I watched videos of sermons by Islamic preachers. Couching their observations in religious terms, people spoke to me about past events, their hopes and personal experiences; the sense of inner peace and order they achieved by hewing to the rules of sharia, and the experience of everyday chaos in Dagestan, which they described in terms of moral decay, social disintegration, and violence.

Against this backdrop of "radical" slogans contained in stories of the present and the past, a picture of complicated local power relations emerged; the sense of exclusion was tied to a strong belief in social justice, a goal that was pursued in the USSR and, it was believed, might be achieved today under an Islamic banner.

From this multitude of visions and convictions emerged the social reality of people who were searching for solutions and trying to reconcile their own experiences of the strong, centralized state that was the USSR with the chaos of the two post-Soviet decades. Instead of the menacing Islamists whose only audible presence in the public sphere took the form of radical slogans, and against whom my secular Makhachkala friends had warned me, I saw people who wished to live in a safe state in which their everyday lives were not governed by corruption and "arrangements." The USSR was once such a state—one that is still remembered or lives on in the recollections of older Dagestanis; today, these aspirations are embodied in the vision of a local Islamic state.

In this chapter, I explain how popular support for Islamic law and so-called radical slogans demanding change in the spirit of Islam are not manifestations of resistance against the state, but paradoxically, actions undertaken out of concern for that very state (with due consideration of how the concept of the state is understood locally). The main target of criticism is not the action of the state but its "inaction" and specifically practices that are perceived to be manifestations of its weakness: corruption, red tape, economic chaos, and the destitution of society. The visions and ideas for change preached by Dagestani Muslims are therefore a response to the state violence; they attempt to answer the questions: How does one live in a place where violence has become a permanent fixture of everyday life? How does a person make the best of his or her life in the face of instability and injustice? Many narratives stress a sense of concern for Russia and Dagestan. They do not challenge the concept of the state itself. Many people emphasized their shared Soviet past, the common goal of freedom for which they fought together in the Great Patriotic War; they bring up stories of their military service, and photos of sons who served or are currently serving in the military are proudly displayed alongside Mecca calendars and pictures of Imam Shamil. At the same time, many of their everyday actions reinterpret the loyalty and concern for the state professed in their narratives. Although inconsistent with a person's professed convictions, these actions are not indications of resistance, cynicism, or hypocrisy. As Alexei Yurchak (2006) demonstrates, citizens of socialist states would break rules that stemmed from the official ideology but without necessarily questioning that ideology. Thus, the transgression of norms should not be associated with acts of resistance. A person could genuinely support the official ideology while acting in a manner that was inconsistent with its tenets; this was recognized by others as an act of reproducing an individual's social status and was not necessarily associated with the literal meaning of the message (283–89). As I explain below, a similar dynamic, to a certain degree, can be observed in the actions undertaken by Dagestani Muslims.

Islam and Sharia in the Narratives of Dagestani Muslims

The narratives shared by Dagestani Muslims contained frequent references to Islamic law, to what some people viewed as the ideal order guaranteed by an Islamic state. Before I explore in greater detail the visions and ideas presented by my subjects, it is worth considering what sharia and Islam mean in the narratives of these individuals. Essentialist depictions of the characteristics of Muslims and their faith are particularly present in scholarship on Islam conducted by Western scholars of the East. However, Muslims should not be treated as products of Islam—individuals defined by their Muslim faith—but as human beings who consider themselves Muslims (Marranci 2020). One cannot understand Muslims based solely on a reading of the Koran, just as it seems inadequate to base one's understanding of Muslims' actions on the nature of Islam and the history of the Muslim world and to subsequently extrapolate that knowledge onto the modern-day practices of believers, as Samuel Huntington (2007) and Bernard Lewis (2004) do. "It is not Islam that shapes Muslims, but rather Muslims who, through discourses, practices, beliefs and actions, make Islam," Marranci (2020, 15) writes; we may agree with the author and nevertheless argue that his conclusion is too strong: in order for Muslims to "make Islam," they must already have been shaped by something else. It seems reasonable to approach Islam as a framework that must be studied, as it facilitates, or perhaps even enables, our understanding of the world and people in question; it should therefore be treated as a map that guides us through the world of our interviewees (15–16), rather than as an ideal model against which to measure other versions of Islam that are sometimes seen as diverging from the norm.

In his book *Islam Obscured*, Daniel Varisco (2005) points out that even descriptions of this framework are not axiologically neutral. Many textbooks assume a markedly Western perspective by describing Islam as a religion that unites people through practice rather than a shared faith (Smith 1991). Books about Islam often open with a description of the five pillars of the faith. Aside from the *shahada* (testimony of faith), the four remaining pillars: prayer (*salah*), alms giving (*zakat*), fasting (*sawm*), and pilgrimage (*hajj*) are simply duties or symbolic actions that tell us little about the message of Islam. It would be more appropriate, Varisco writes, to begin by stating that Islam is a monotheistic religion, Muhammad is its prophet, and the Koran deals with matters of morality, the struggle between good and evil, the rising of the dead, the day of judgment, relations between men and women, and other practical aspects of everyday life.

Two phrases that I often heard used interchangeably in conversations about Islam in Dagestan were "living according to Islam" (*zhit' po islamu*) and "living according to sharia" (*zhit' po sharyatu*); this typically meant adherence to particular principles that were context dependent and subject to reinterpretation but which drew on both the local social reality and Islamic law as laid out in the Koran and the hadith. What does sharia mean in the theological tradition of Islam, and what areas of life does it regulate?

The Koran and the hadith form the foundation of what Muslims call sharia, or Islamic law. The hadith, or narratives about the life and actions of the prophet, are the basis of the sunna, which is considered by Muslims to be the most important source for sharia, after the Koran. Initially transmitted orally, the hadith began to "multiply uncontrollably" after the death of the prophet, leading Muslim scholars to assign each to one of four groups: authentic, good, weak, and fabricated (Hallaq 1999).

Sharia regulates many aspects of a person's everyday life: rituals associated with everything from birth and circumcision to weddings and funerals. It also regulates family and community relations. In the case of an event (e.g., a conflict) whose solution is not determined by the Koran or the sunna, the parties may request the individual opinion, or *ijtihad*, of a scholar, who reaches a verdict using the Koran and hadith. However, individual opinions have led to disagreements (*khilaf*) in the past. New laws were thus recognized as valid only when they resulted in consensus (*ijma*). Khilaf resulted in the formation of many separate schools of thought, or madhhabs: Hanafi, Maliki, Shafi'i, and Hanbali, each of which bears the name of its founder.

The Caucasus is home to two schools: Shafi'i (Dagestan, Chechnya, and Ingushetia) and Hanafi (North Dagestan, particularly areas inhabited by the Nogais, and the western part of the North Caucasus). Much of the scholarship on Islam in the North Caucasus begins with the history of Islamization, describing the influence of individual schools and streams of Islam. Meanwhile, few of my subjects were even aware of the madhhabs, much less of the differences among them. Despite their involvement in religious practices, some of my subjects had not even thought about whether they considered themselves Sunni or Shia.

Learning about the individual religious practices of the faithful allowed me to better understand my Dagestani subjects and, more broadly, relationships of power in the Russian Caucasus.

There are many interpretations of Islam, just as there are many personal embodiments of Islam and Islamic law. However, only after we become acquainted with the testimonies of individual people who explain what the terms *Islam* and *sharia* mean to them (among them Rustam, Abdul-Hamid, Imam of Tindi, and Jamilat, whose narratives and experiences I explore below), can we examine these concepts as part of a greater social reality. My subjects learned about Islam and sharia from many different sources, as did I. Their knowledge and the knowledge of the people they encountered were subject to constant reinterpretation.

Even when my subjects referred to similar theological frameworks, it cannot be assumed that they experienced the same Islam—embodied Islam.

In what terms did Abdul-Hamid, Jamilat, Imam of Tindi, Rizvan, and Rustam speak about Islam and sharia when they talked about their visions of the future? What experiences did they refer to? Which elements of sharia did they emphasize and consider the most important?

Comprehensive Projects, Personal Projects, Community Projects

Although my experiences in the field were limited to secular Makhachkala, I observed, noted, and described visions presented by Dagestani Muslims, paying most attention to clear, radical statements and declarations in an attempt to assign them (and by extension, my subjects) to one of the binary categories employed by the media: Wahhabis and Tariqatists. I gradually discovered, however, that those radical slogans were tied to experiences and notions of a Soviet past that found a distinctive reflection in visions for the new Islamic future of Dagestan.

My conversations, interviews, experiences, and observations of the social reality of religious Dagestan gradually revealed the existence of three attitudes, three visions of change: comprehensive visions, in the spirit of large-scale modernization projects, involving ideas for reforming society as a whole; community visions, which emphasized the urgency of restoring order within the jamaat; and personal visions, which were geared toward gradual reforms in a person's own life. Even though these visions of change could be described as reform projects, I deliberately avoid this term due to potential direct associations with Islamic reformism, which would imply that the projects were religious, rather than political, in nature.

I selected the following conversations and accounts of situations and experiences from among many others, not all of which were similar to these. Gathering knowledge and experience over the course of several years forced me to continuously reevaluate the opinions and interpretation at which I had previously arrived; I deliberately make no secret of this. However, in order to paint a fuller picture of this process, I refer here to my conversations with people such as Abdul-Hamid, Jamilat, and Huseyn, whom I also write about elsewhere in this book, in order to provide readers with a more thorough understanding of the dilemmas each person faced and to offer them greater insight into the lives of my subjects and, by extension, the problems I discuss here. I cite extensive fragments in contexts that are not always pertinent to this particular chapter but that are nevertheless relevant to the book as a whole.

Comprehensive Projects: "Society Needs a Religious Awakening"

Calls for people to live according to sharia, praise of an Islamic state, and the struggle for the "morality of the nation" were clearly present in the public space in Dagestan. Slogans such as "Fear Allah," "Allah is great," and "Live according to sharia" were appearing on buildings and fences with growing frequency. Faces and uncovered parts of the female body would be painted over on billboards. More and more stores posted signs "We do not sell alcohol." Only larger stores could afford to sell liquor while also paying the extortionists who threatened to burn the building down or plant an explosive device. Open calls for jihad were becoming ever more frequent in the public space, on walls, and on stickers: "Everyone is called to jihad," "Jihad against the infidels." And more and more often, these words could be heard from the mouths of Dagestani Muslims.

"Obscurantism [*mrakobesie*], backwardness, fanaticism, lack of education"—I would hear these words from my subjects in secular, educated Makhachkala when, during our evening conversation, I shared my observations about my encounters with religious Makhachkala. "So they want an Islamic state, do they?," "Idiots are building another caliphate," "Let them live however they please, but don't impose anything on others," "You don't see me out on my balcony at five in the morning yelling, 'There is no god!' at the top of my lungs, but that doesn't keep them from imposing their own order; they scream (call) the *adhan* at 5:00 a.m. and won't let you sleep." With each passing year, my subjects grew increasingly alarmed at the creeping Islamization of the republic and the prospect of an Islamic order.

As I heard people talk daily about sharia, an Islamic state, and the need for radical change, I gradually learned more and more about religious Makhachkala. With time, I had heard enough stories, met enough people, and amassed enough experience to be able to approach these ostensibly radical slogans not through the lens of an orientalized view of Islam, one shaped by the media and books on the fundamentals of Islam, but through the lens of my own experiences with the state, violence, and the experience of life in Dagestan.

Rizvan: "Allah Will Unite All People under the Flag of Socialism"

Mariam, a thirty-one-year-old woman, met Rizvan in the Islamic store where she shopped for black cumin oil (*maslo chornogo tmina*), which is imported from Arab countries and has recently become a prized cure-all. They struck up a conversation about Islamic medicine and the benefits of faith in Allah.

"Rizvan talked to me about Islam, but there was something different, something wiser about how he did it. He didn't say things like, 'You have to wear the hijab. Wearing jeans makes you a prostitute.' Some idiots will say things like that. He said that wearing the hijab is something you have to mature into and that a person's outfit isn't the most important thing: what really matters is what's in your heart. He also said that he couldn't force me to perform salah," Mariam told me. "But then I happened to be holding tickets for a concert I was going to. He started telling me (*gruzit'*) that music was evil and that I shouldn't attend concerts. I didn't want to admit that I was a singer myself." Mariam laughed. "But he also said a lot of wise things, different from what others say. You could tell he had it well thought-out. He read a lot of books. He talked about what was important to him. He encouraged me to gradually convert to Islam. Maybe someday, who knows? You have to meet him."

I met with Rizvan, aged thirty-five, and Mariam for the first time in a café. I do not recall much of our conversation. Rizvan talked about Islam and tried to convert me. He formulated most of his thought around references to the Koran, and I did not understand everything, as I was not familiar with the surahs he was citing. His monotonous voice made me drowsy. He maintained that Islam was healthful for the body as well as the soul and that all good flowed from the Koran. Rizvan did not want me to record our conversation, and I was not able to reconstruct much of it from my notes afterward.

"What did you think when you saw me? That I'm some Wahhabi? I bet you're going to write that you met a bearded Wahhabi," he said as we parted.

"Uh, no, why do you say that?" I asked, even though he was exactly right about my first impression.

Rizvan appeared not to trust me. I did not expect him to want to see me again, nor did I try to set up another conversation. It was Mariam who arranged the next meeting as part of her efforts to help me find interviewees. (Or perhaps it was just an excuse to see Rizvan again. She had not seen him since our previous meeting a few months earlier.) I met with Rizvan for the second time at a café in downtown Makhachkala, where I was joined by Mariam and a female colleague, Iwa Kołodziejska.

"I guess I didn't frighten you too badly, seeing as you agreed to meet again."

"No, I was very interested in what you had to say," I replied, just to say something.

"What exactly did you find interesting?"

"Well, you know, the stuff you said about Islam," I answered unconvincingly, relying on my scant memories of our previous encounter.

Rizvan made conversation. "You're Christians, right? Christianity has gone down the wrong path. You believe in the Holy Trinity? Don't know you that's *shirk*? God cannot exist in three forms."

Iwa tried to debate him. "That's not exactly right."

"But there's only one God. You can't add associates onto him."

"Well, no, that's . . ." I tried to explain.

"Why do you need all these novelties? In Islam, everything is simple. There's one God and no intermediaries. The whole world is slowly converting to Islam. Jean-Michel Cousteau accepted Islam. Even Michael Jackson was a Muslim. It's not just Russia: it's the whole world! People are finally starting to understand. Everyone is born a Muslim; it's only later that they're shaped by their environment."

Rizvan was clearly most interested in having a discussion about Christianity and trying to convert us to Islam. Meanwhile, I was more interested in learning how he envisaged the future of his republic and what he thought about an Islamic state. I tried to divert our conversation onto a different track.

I nodded even when I disagreed with his views. I inquired about the situation in Dagestan.

"There's a war of ideologies going on. A war between truth and falsehood. We're fighting for the truth. All of humanity is moving forward [*k progresu*], there's progress. And it will eventually reach the truth. One day the truth [*istina*] will prevail and everyone will find their own way to Islam. Things will be better when they follow the instructions of the prophet. It's all there in the Koran. We're halfway there now. There's still a long road to victory."

"What happens when you achieve victory?" I asked.

"There will be unity and unanimity."

"I see. . . . And what about the state?" I clearly assumed that Rizvan was referring to a separatist Islamic state or Caucasus Emirate.

"Hmm . . . the state is built on the wrong foundations. But look, you already have Islamic banks. That's a start. These banks operate without committing usury."

"And what schools and institutions would replace those provided by the state?" I asked.

"There are madrassas. But secular schools aren't that bad. You have to study. It's just that those schools don't provide the right foundations."

"Aren't you worried that if they win, everything will be a mess?"

"No, then there will be unity. The Koran is our 'antivirus.' You can't have anyone governing the slaves of Allah. We still don't have a leader of truth. There are only imams in the mosques. . . . Caucasian Islam is the proudest. We need to strive for a unified Islam. There should be no differences. Cosmopolitanism is good. We should adopt the best things that others have. The Dagestani model is good: we have so many different nationalities here, and we can already see that nations will quietly disappear. Socialism is the first step, an example of how to live as brothers. It's the first step toward unification. Allah united the people under the flag of socialism, only last time it was based on materialism. But the very fact of unification is important because it shows how important unity is. Allah saved the Russians. If they had not united, they would no longer exist," Rizvan said and added, "Even Hitler said so."

I was initially hesitant to bring up what I believed to the delicate subject of how this vision would be carried out in practice. I wondered how violence fit into it. I was also unsure of the degree of Rizvan's support for the methods commonly used by militants, which included acts of violence against policemen, businessmen, civil servants, and people involved in esoteric practices. I was afraid that this question would cause Rizvan to suspect, correctly, that I thought his views radical.

Mariam's long-haired friend Artyom briefly joined the conversation. The young man criticized Rizvan's ideas for the future of Dagestan outright, calling them utopian, fanatical, and backward. It appeared that Artyom and Rizvan had had this debate before. Being careful not to support the arguments of either side, I decided to ask about the recent spate of murders of fortune-tellers (once again drawing on my knowledge of so-called Wahhabi practices—information that I had gleaned from websites and analytical reports).

"[Killing fortune-tellers] is necessary for our future development [evolution]. Divination is forbidden. Those charlatans get their knowledge from the devil. That's probably how they can foretell the future and predict the situations we encounter. But it is up to us to find our own solutions to these situations. We're supposed to build our own future for the truth. The Koran protects us against charlatanism."

"Do you think they should be murdered?" I asked.

"I'm not against it," Rizvan said cautiously. "They don't just kill everyone indiscriminately. They warn them first. Fortune-tellers and other charlatans simply have a different view of the truth than we do, and we try to lead them to the truth. Take Daniil Sysoyev, for example. They warned him several times before they finally killed him. Serves him right, the fool [*durachok*]."

"Why do the militants extort jihad money from businessmen? Doesn't Islam forbid it?"

"You mean racketeering? They should pay up. The people being extorted are enemies of the truth. As far as truth goes, they live by different laws. We try to bring them over to our side and convince them of the truth."

"By extorting them? Then you're not that different from them. You use the same methods," I said candidly. By that time, I had stopped worrying about what Rizvan would think and had begun to speak my mind.

A similar comparison to members of an organized crime syndicate was made by Charles Tilly (1985) in reference to former colonial states. He argues that these governments effectively run a racket, particularly when it comes to collecting "donations" for protection (provision of protection). The criminal underworld pretends to be the government when collecting dues in return for which it promises protection and social order.

Rizvan fell silent. I was afraid that I might have reacted too sharply to his words and that he was now sulking. Then again, he had upset me and I could not simply respond to everything he said with a nod. I was also curious how he would react to the comparison. But Rizvan then began to ask me what I thought of Dagestan. I told him frankly what I thought of the situation in the republic, sparing no criticism of the authorities or the militants.

"You know a lot," Rizvan remarked as I went on about Dagestan. These words typically preceded a series of questions about what I was doing there, who was paying me, and whether it was the U.S. Department of State. But Rizvan was silent.

I was rescued from the awkward silence by Mariam, who had hardly said a word during our discussion and, two hours in, was growing weary. She suggested that we take a walk to the seaside. Mariam discreetly paid the bill and told Rizvan that the café was run by her friends, implying that the tea was free. She later explained that neither she nor we could have openly paid for the tea, and she knew that Rizvan had no money. "He would have been offended," she explained. "In Dagestan, it's not customary for women to pay for men, and of course guests never pay," she added. "But you know that."

Rizvan was silent during the walk. I gradually realized how my questions had placed him within the Sufi-Wahhabi dichotomy. He had been one of the first people to speak openly about the need to achieve change by "fighting for the truth," which I assumed to mean violent struggle. It is possible, however, that he had only begun to consider some of topics we discussed, such as fortune-telling and racketeering, during our conversation.

"It was nice talking to you. Maybe we'll meet again," Rizvan offered as we parted ways. "You're kind of right about Dagestan," he admitted.

When talking to Rizvan, I did not assume the stance of the astute interviewer who nods and asks the occasional question, as I usually did when interviewing subjects, encouraging them to speak their mind without challenging them or judging their views. By openly expressing my own opinions, I earned Rizvan's trust rather than provoking his ire; he began to see me as a conversation partner, a person with whom he could examine his own worldview. This research encounter helped me understand that in a context so deeply marked by violence and conflict, assuming a neutral stance (if that is even possible) can raise a series of suspicions about the researcher's "indifferent" position (as was the case with me).

Rustam: "Our Society Doesn't Provide the Necessary Conditions for Development"

"I'll be there in half an hour," Abdul-Hamid told me over the phone. "I have a reading, and they agreed," he added with his usual brevity. The conversation was quick. "Readings"—shorthand for exorcisms—are usually held in the homes of people who require this sort of treatment.

I was greeted at the door by a middle-aged man; his name, I learned later, was Rustam. He came across as a very serious and distrustful person, one who was not quite comfortable with the presence of camera-wielding strangers in his mother's house. Nonetheless, when the exorcism was over (see the section "The Story of Amina: Conflicts in the Body" in chapter 2), he invited us to stay for tea and talk. We wanted to talk about jinns, but Rustam got into a conversation with Abdul-Hamid, in fact, launching into a long monologue directed at him as well as—or perhaps especially for—the camera. He was pleased with our interest in Islam and was glad that we wanted to shoot a film. I almost did not have to ask questions.

"I was fifty years old when I started praying," Rustam recalled. "I'm fifty-eight now. No-one forced me to take the faith. When I was forty, I began searching for something. For nearly ten years, my heart was full of hatred and bitterness over my failed business and my family problems. And I thought to myself, 'How could I, a person with such hatred in my heart pray?' Ten years later, someone told me, 'Draw the line here. Remember this, and leave that behind. Just forget it. And from this day forward, always try to act righteously.'"

"Mom, don't interrupt! Give us a minute!" Rustam scolded his elderly mother when she attempted, once again, to bring in what we later learned was not tea but dinner. He returned to his monologue. "I have two degrees, one in medicine and the other in finance, and now I want to attend Islamic university in the evening to learn more about my religion so that I can share my faith in God with at least one person."

Rustam had been working as a doctor for thirty years. He also ran his own business and admitted that he had not always been an honest businessman.

"I look forward to the day when there are hardly any hypocrites. They're the worst type of people. Even the infidels are a thousand times better! I have many weaknesses myself. I believe I'm still in an underclass of Islam. I still have much to learn. Pride can make a person stop learning. God gave us the right to choose: we can learn good or evil."

"Back in the days of the communists . . ." Rustam continued. "It's true that the communists killed my grandfather, but in those days, people had a pension and could help their children out. And now? Do you think I can help? Worst of all is the social injustice. That didn't happen under communism. If someone makes little money these days, they say, 'How are you supposed to live righteously? You can't take bribes!' If you're a moral person, you know that these circumstances, this whole mess is just a period of trial and temptation. Whatever the circumstances, people should always seek a solution that is pleasing to God. That's more difficult than submitting to your emotions and saying, 'I'll do this and change it.' They blame everything on Islamic extremism. That's just a cover. The real problem is always social injustice. If you look at the Irish and the Basques, you'll see that it's always social injustice, not religion, that pushes people toward extremism."

"Our society doesn't provide the necessary conditions for development. Young people think to themselves, 'Why am I worse off than the rich man?' And then it's easy to lead them down the garden path. They are like half-filled bookshelves. Society is supposed to take responsibility for young people, but it's given up on that effort. Young people are flooded with a stream of information, but there's no filter—they don't know how to pick out the knowledge that is true.... Censorship—we need censorship. You can't show on television that people can commit crimes with impunity. If society doesn't assume responsibility, then young people will accept negative information of all sorts. You need to have a spiritual filter. Society needs to tend to the souls of its youth. We were created as social beings, but if society doesn't create laws that fulfill our spiritual needs, a conflict will break out between society and its members. People need to be enlightened."

"A person with moral principles who fears God is better, is good for all governments and all systems, because he fears the Creator. When a criminal breaks the law, he thinks he's gotten away with something, that he can escape justice. But you can't hide from God. There was once an *alim* who had students. They asked him, 'Why do you favor one student? What makes him better?' 'Come,' he said, 'and see for yourselves.' He tell the students to kill a bird. Each of them killed a bird—except for the one student. 'I couldn't find a place to hide from the eyes of God.' When there's more people like that, it'll be easier to obey the law, and things will be better in every country. The believer is responsible because he knows that he will be punished and that he will answer to God for his every word. If we choose the path of good and righteousness, we will answer to Allah, our families, and society."

"There is a war being waged for minds, hearts, and spirits. That's why true believers, the slaves of the Almighty, cannot be slaves to circumstance. Society has forgotten about this. The weaker the rules, the more weak, immoral, and stupid slaves he wants to have. People like that can't tell him that his state doesn't fulfill people's basic needs. Society should educate its members and have expectations. If it educates without expecting anything, then it's a mess.... Human life is like the life of a fly: it has no value in Dagestan. Buying and selling is all that matters. Society needs to think about turning to God. You can't treat a person like a machine, turning his heart this way and that. People need to have morals. If we want a better world, our human laws will have to be subordinate to divine law, not the other way around.... Allah gave us laws to guide our lives, and there can be no law or ideology better than the law of Allah. There is wisdom in each of Allah's laws. You might not immediately comprehend the benefits of his proscriptions, but you'll understand eventually. There is no better law than divine law, nor can there be."

"Muhammad created religion. And when Americans tested the relevance of various religions, the computers always put Muhammad in first place. And what does modern society put in first place? Power, strength, money. That's a feature of polytheism. . . . The very word *Allah*—and scientist have proved this—is good for your body; goodness flows from it."

"Right, that's why jinns fear the word *Allah*," Abdul-Hamid adds.

"Even if you take so-called traditional medicine, if it offers comfort, then go ahead and use vitamins, all kinds of medicine; you can't reject that. That comes from Allah as well. Nothing we do happens without his knowledge. You can't say, 'This is bad, now only so-called nontraditional medicine is good.' I'm a doctor and I know that some patients look like they're beyond treatment and yet they survive, and some people aren't that sick and yet they die. We can't explain that. Everything happens because of Allah's will."

"There are many different nations in Dagestan, and each contributes something to society. Each nation has its own traditions. Tradition, when it is not at odds with Islam, when the adat does not violate sharia, carries no harmful consequences. But when someone is mature and you tell them they're making a mistake, and they say, 'What do you know? You're young.' . . . It's not good that people don't take an interest [in these matters]. That's why we have this mess [*bardak*]. The DUMD forbids translations of the Koran, but not everyone can learn Arabic. There are translations, so why not use them? Why not read with comprehension? That's a foolish crowd mentality. . . . Our clerics publish their own books. They even said that if you reject the *tariqa*, then you're an atheist—that's their logic. And then they put these people in FSB [Federal Security Service] units, the FSB authorities, and they start working on that there. They spend tons of money on those units, and they work and work against the stream. But when someone needs some form of treatment, they refer them to people like me. They can't do it themselves. The only treatment they can offer is to write out a slip of paper [*bumazhka*] and say, 'Use this as a talisman and everything will be good.' And if you read these talismans, you'll see that there's plenty of unnecessary stuff in there."

Abdul-Hamid interrupts him. "It's time for salah. Let us pray," he says, looking at his watch.

"If we said anything wrong, may God forgive us and give us the strength to live on this earth. And we thank you for not being indifferent to what happens in this world," Rustam says as he leaves the kitchen with Abdul-

Hamid. We sit down to eat the meal that Rustam's mother has been trying to serve us.

Slogans about social development, calls to lead a moral life, and the demand that the state police the morality of individuals (particularly the youth) were frequently mentioned in the narratives of Dagestani Muslims.

Like Rizvan, some of my subjects believed the situation could not be changed without violence, while others, including Rustam, condemned the use of force, preferring to "convert society" gradually. It is notable that in their criticisms of the current situation in the republic, both Rustam and Rizvan contrasted it not only with an ideal state inhabited by religious Muslims but also with the ideal just state, as many people who shared their views believed the USSR to be.

The experience of Soviet modernization—or rather, the social memory of modernization—has clearly and strongly influenced the way in which the inhabitants of the former USSR would like their future, their state, and their society to be. Criticism of the Soviet period was directed not at socialist ideals but at the incompetent execution of specific projects. Even if the premises of the Soviet project were never fully realized, there was a conviction that these dreams could still come true—perhaps in a different, better system.

As a result of the modernization practices and methods of action employed by the Soviet state, many people in the former USSR perceived themselves to be modern. They saw themselves as citizens of a superpower, a country in which much had changed in recent years. This was particularly significant and apparent on the margins of the Soviet Union, in places such as the Caucasus and Central Asia. The ethic of a self-improving, purpose-driven community was central to the development of many individuals' worldview and self-perception. Another important factor was the effort to create a new, better person, a new society. Subjects emphasized values such as gender equality, the eradication of illiteracy, and work guided by a greater goal. These ideals were particularly present in the narratives of party members whose statements centered on the future.

Many of my subjects contrasted Soviet modernization with the period following the collapse of the USSR, which they referred to as capitalism. In the view of local residents, post-Soviet capitalism gradually came to resemble capitalism as it was portrayed by Soviet propaganda, rather than the system they encountered in the movies, music, and other desirable and awe-inspiring goods that filtered through the Iron Curtain. Perestroika and the years following the fall of the USSR, which ended in disillusionment, were often contrasted with the Soviet times—a period of modernization, "modernity," and progress.

The experience of Western-style modernization never became the experience of post-Soviet Muslims. Westernization was looked at ambivalently in Soviet times: on the one hand, it was perceived negatively as a threat to Soviet values and structures, but on the other hand, particularly in the period of perestroika, it was lauded for its progress and the better tomorrow promised by unattainable goods. However, this was an imagined reality rather than an experienced one, as the material goods that began streaming in from the West were beyond the reach of most citizens. Western modernity was only accessible to a select few; for most people, it remained an object of dreams and desires but not experience, while they increasingly perceived their own lives in terms of demodernization. In effect, it was not Western modernization that became the object of criticism but the status quo that required modernization in the realms of the economy, morality, and society, which had been eroding since the fall of the USSR.

Rustam's and Rizvan's narratives reveal a distinct longing for an ethic in which society is seen as a group of people who share a common goal; a community that shapes individuals, influences their morality and knowledge, and encourages their self-improvement. Both refer to notions of the state and society under the USSR and to the concept of individual evolutionary stages through which nations were believed to progress (from this perspective, the current conflict is simply one stage of development). Rizvan and Rustam also mention widespread and strongly internalized notions of modernization and progress interrupted by periods of chaos. Both projects are built on the belief that Islamization is the next "positive" stage after socialism. As with revolution, this process requires a great deal of work and even sacrifice. They dream of reforms that would change human habits and patterns of behavior. These are radical, comprehensive changes. Also notable is their future-oriented thinking, which was characteristic of the Soviet period (and is echoed in statements made by Russian authorities today). To put it in more figurative terms, one might draw an analogy to the twentieth-century modernization projects described by James Scott (1998), which were intended to raise living standards through comprehensive solutions such as collectivization, the construction of villages, and compulsory "villagization" in Tanzania. All of these solutions were schematic and ignored the characteristics of actual social orders that were uncodified and relied on informal processes and improvisation (4–6), leading, as Scott demonstrates, to their ultimate failure.

One important element in the narratives of many Dagestani Muslims who, like Rizvan and Rustam, presented visions of radical and comprehensive change, was the struggle for "social morality." Issues such as women's clothing and morality were discussed with growing frequency, especially after the so-called sauna incident. In August 2009, a group of militants raided a sauna (a euphemism for brothels used widely throughout Dagestan and many other parts of the former USSR) in Buynaksk, killing seven prostitutes and several policemen from the nearby precinct. The officers were said to have been running a racket, extorting money from the brothel in exchange for permitting the illegal operation to continue. The raid drew praise from both secular and religious Dagestan. The militants' actions were framed as "laying down the law" and "rooting out chaos and debauchery" (as one sixty-five-year-old man put it), especially after it was revealed that the women employed at the brothel had been from Dagestan and were not, as had widely been assumed, Russians or Ukrainians. Following this event, my subjects began to speak more positively about the efforts undertaken by Ramzan Kadyrov in neighboring Chechnya. Local media described the measures in question as "the implementation of elements of sharia"; they included a mandate that women wear headscarves in public places, a ban on the sale of alcohol during Ramadan or outside of certain hours in other months, and a crackdown on brothels and gambling (see figure 5.1). Kadyrov commanded the respect of many of my Dagestani subjects, who saw him as someone who could instill order in the republic and whose effectiveness was apparent in the modestly dressed women and clean streets. Chechnya's cleanliness was contrasted with the dirtiness of Dagestan. Ignored in the past, the garbage that littered the streets, rivers, and lakes became a sign of the ineffectiveness of the state and its indifference to its citizens. Rather than hide their own garbage from the eyes of a foreigner (a practice I encountered in 2004–2008), Dagestanis would draw my attention to litter (pointing out, for example, plastic bags that had been swept up by the wind and wound up in trees and bushes), complain about cows roaming the streets, and emphasize the urgent need to implement changes, "instill order," and impose sharia. People would say, "Ramzan is a fine man [*molodets*]; he's imposing sharia and doesn't care what Moscow thinks" (male, about thirty years old). "He cares about his nation and he's a practicing Muslim" (male, about fifty years old). "Look how clean it is in Chechnya. They rebuilt everything" (male, about forty years old). "They say there are no saunas in Chechnya, and all the women wear headscarves. You have to give credit where credit is due: he led the republic out of war" (male, about fifty years old). "If they catch a government minister taking bribes, they fire him" (male, about forty years old). The calls for sharia or an Islamic state present in the "comprehensive projects" were often veiled forms of practices that had been widespread in the Soviet Union, such as the emphasis on producing moral citizens, cleanliness—in the broadest sense of the term—and the notion of prioritizing the group over the individual.

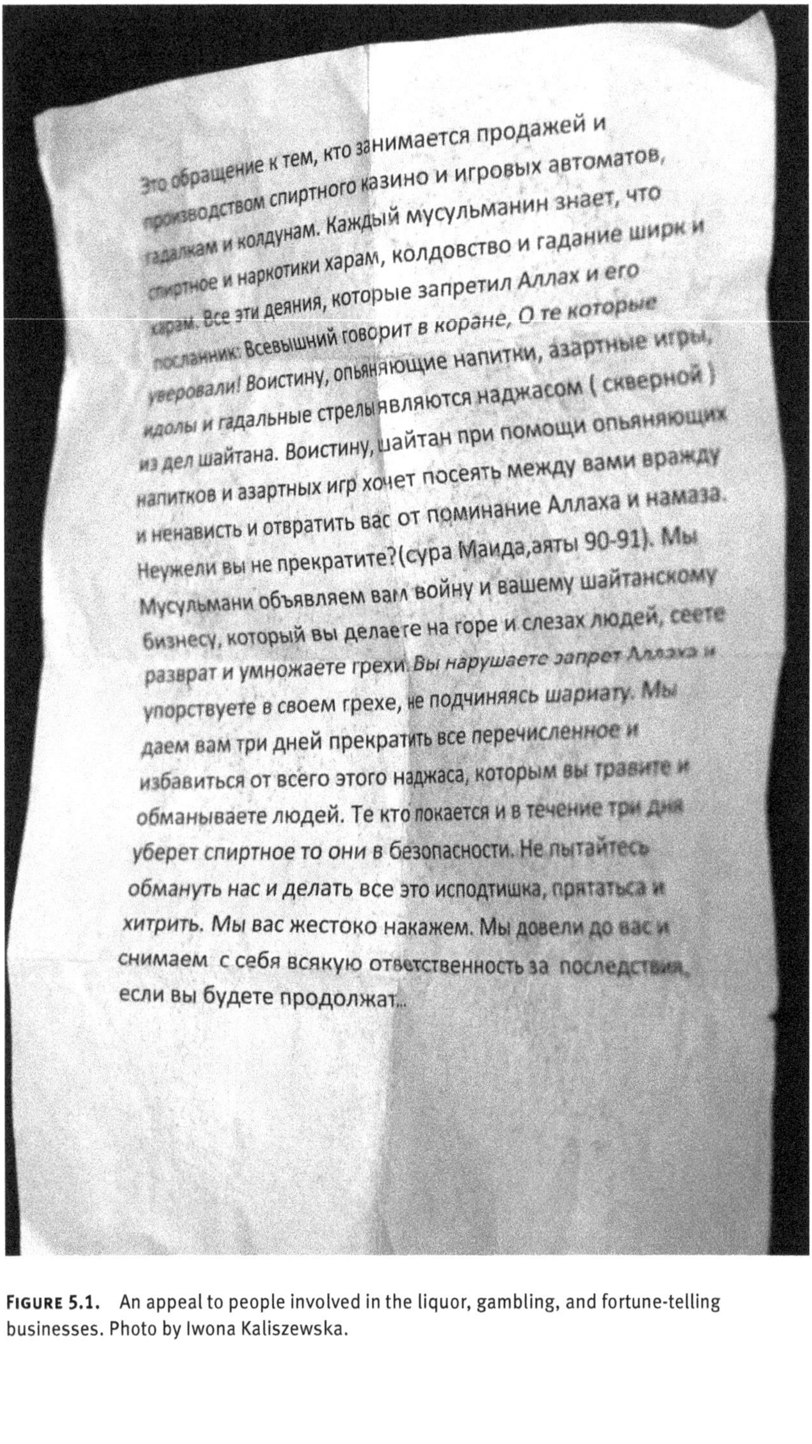

Это обращение к тем, кто занимается продажей и производством спиртного казино и игровых автоматов, гадалкам и колдунам. Каждый мусульманин знает, что спиртное и наркотики харам, колдовство и гадание ширк и харам. Все эти деяния, которые запретил Аллах и его посланник: Всевышний говорит в коране, О те которые уверовали! Воистину, опьяняющие напитки, азартные игры, идолы и гадальные стрелы являются наджасом (скверной) из дел шайтана. Воистину, шайтан при помощи опьяняющих напитков и азартных игр хочет посеять между вами вражду и ненависть и отвратить вас от поминание Аллаха и намаза. Неужели вы не прекратите?(сура Маида,аяты 90-91). Мы Мусульмани объявляем вам войну и вашему шайтанскому бизнесу, который вы делаете на горе и слезах людей, сеете разврат и умножаете грехи. Вы нарушаете запрет Аллаха и упорствуете в своем грехе, не подчиняясь шариату. Мы даем вам три дней прекратить все перечисленное и избавиться от всего этого наджаса, которым вы травите и обманываете людей. Те кто покается и в течение три дня уберет спиртное то они в безопасности. Не пытайтесь обмануть нас и делать все это исподтишка, прятаться и хитрить. Мы вас жестоко накажем. Мы довели до вас и снимаем с себя всякую ответственность за последствия, если вы будете продолжат...

FIGURE 5.1. An appeal to people involved in the liquor, gambling, and fortune-telling businesses. Photo by Iwona Kaliszewska.

Personal Visions: Sharia at Home

It was not uncommon in the 1990s for people to carry out radical changes in their personal lives, explore their spirituality, and join religious groups. Among my interviewees in secular Makhachkala, the turn toward Islam was initially regarded similarly to the newfound interest in the Baha'i faith, Hare Krishna, Vissarionites, yoga, and health food. New converts emphasized the "naturalness" of their religious practices and their beneficial effects on a person's health and well-being.

"Sharia Is the Most Natural Law There Is": Abdul-Hamid's Story

I was introduced to Abdul-Hamid, a man in his early thirties, by his wife's sister, who worked at the Islamic store in my neighborhood. He specialized in Islamic medicine, which included hijama (medicinal bloodletting or wet cupping) and expelling jinns. He also ran a small Islamic shop carrying a wide selection of religious literature, DVDs, clothing, and cosmetics—products imported from Arab countries, along with their local counterparts. I hung around the store, chatting with Abdul-Hamid and his customers. I also tried to accompany him to exorcisms—which he called "readings" in reference to reading the Koran—in order to learn more about his friends and clients. These people lived in different parts of Makhachkala, but they had many experiences in common and shared a number of similar views on society. Some of them were Abdul-Hamid's direct acquaintances or friends of friends, while others, particularly those who came for only hijama, were complete strangers. Along with Abdul-Hamid and his customers, I talked to other salesmen and the faithful who spent lots of time in the neighborhood surrounding the mosque.

Abdul-Hamid usually performed the hijama procedure at the store (see figure 5.2), though he did do the occasional house call. Readings mostly took place in the home of the person possessed by jinns.

I sat in the prayer room adjoining Abdul-Hamid's store (which doubled as a space for hijama treatment) and listened as he told me about his life, sharia, Islam, and how hard it was to live in Dagestan.

"The Koran tells us how to live. It's a constitution," he explained. "One constitution is sharia, a set of instructions for God-fearing people. It is written in the Koran: He who does not follow the commandments of Allah is an infidel. If a person chooses to live according to a different constitution, whatever it may be—a criminal ideology or *poniatiya* [criminal code] but not Islam and says that

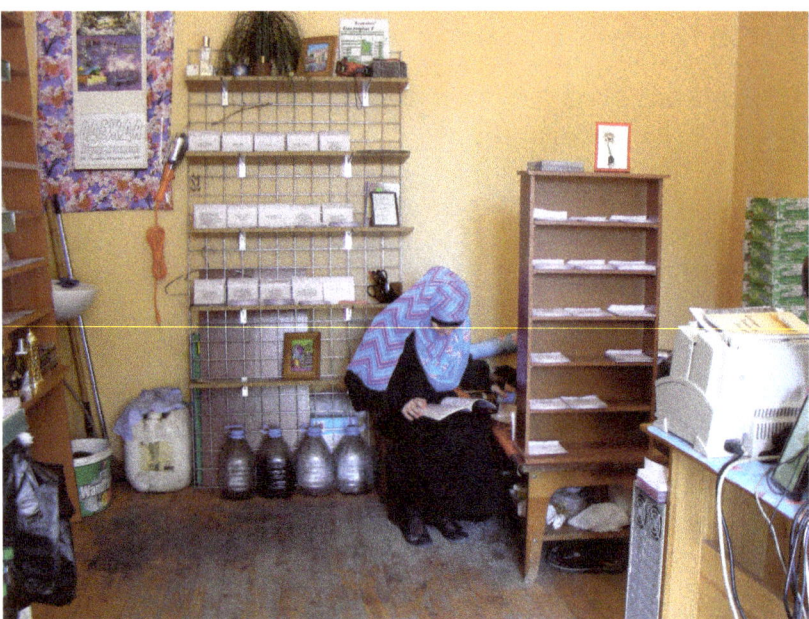

FIGURE 5.2.   Islamic store and *hijama* practice in Makhachkala. Photo by Iwona Kaliszewska.

he will live according to it—then he is automatically banished from the religious sphere. In the Koran, in the *ayat*, it is written, 'Do you not seek better laws?'"

"And how are we supposed to obey the law in Dagestan? How are we supposed to live here? If a person follows the law of Allah, he will be happy, both in medical terms and in other ways. [It is unclear what my subject has in mind here.] Even using a miswak stick is beneficial. Every movement in prayer, performing the ablution—all of these provide benefits," Abdul-Hamid said, handing me the miswak stick he had retrieved from a drawer a moment earlier. "The Prophet Muhammad said, 'Wear a beard, shave your mustache.' I walk down the street and people stare at me. They call me a Wahhabi. Wahhab is the sixteenth name of Allah, and look what they do: they try to insult me by calling me the name of Allah. They will answer for that on the day of judgment. Scientists have proved that if four generations of men shave their facial hair, then the next generations will be of a nontraditional orientation because the male hormones will be replaced with female ones. That's what happens when men keep shaving. I was reading the Koran to one girl, and the jinn came out and said, 'How do you like our advertising slogan, *Gillette, the best a man can get*?' That's all their doing."

"Allah created the whole world, except for toilets and saunas," Abdul-Hamid continued. "Allah made many things much simpler. For example, it is forbidden to eat pork. Why? Because it brings you no benefit, only harm. And one more thing. Scientists have explained why it's good to eat mutton. By eating mutton, you absorb its character, its jealousy. And when you eat pork, you get indifference and a bland character, like Russians. If you've never felt jealousy, you won't go to heaven. I don't mean you have to be jealous about your wife. But you have to protect her. For example, I always walk my wife to the marshrutka and make sure she gets a seat with the women. I don't want her to have to sit next to a man. That sort of jealousy is acceptable."

"Women here don't have to cover up. Well, maybe just a little, for the sake of modesty. You're dressed all right, more or less," he said, gesturing toward my jeans and long blouse. "And what do they do around here? They wear skirts up to here." Abdul-Hamid pointed to his upper thigh. "Then those girls find themselves dragged into a car, and they wonder why. . . . They just provoke bad thoughts in men. Allah placed men higher because they have more responsibility. It is the men, not the women, who will be held responsible for the mess we have here. If I want my woman—my wife, that is—to dress modestly, then she covers up. But that isn't the norm here. They even look at you funny in the marshrutka, especially when a woman is dressed in all black. The neighbors stare at us, too. But Allah said that women should wear dark colors to avoid drawing attention to themselves."

"The law of the state was invented by people, and they live according to that law. Endless amendments, endless red tape. Let's say, for example, that I want to buy some land. Nothing grows there. Well, then you need to pay this amount in bribes! According to sharia, you can come and take a piece. And how does it work in Dagestan? I bought some land and plans. And then the papers went missing. They just sold the same plot of land to someone else! They do that to extort money. 'What do you mean the papers are missing?' I asked. 'I've got the document right here in my hand!' 'It's just gone. That's it,' they said. And you just keep on paying."

"You can't live and work in peace here. They [the security forces, the police] know what I do for a living, and still they keep showing up, knocking at my door at six in the morning to search my home. They won't leave me alone."

"There will be no peace in Dagestan until there is justice. . . . But there will be justice soon enough, *inshallah*."

At our later interviews, Abdul-Hamid talked a lot about his work. He was very busy, and it was difficult to set an appointment with him. On Tuesdays and Thursday, he performed hijamas all day long (see figure 5.3). He used a special set of cups brought over from Saudi Arabia. He talked a lot about the benefits of Islamic medicine and how widespread medicinal bloodletting was, and he encouraged me to try the treatment for myself. "It works on Christians, too," he laughed.

"They've even started performing hijama in Saint Petersburg. It's now an official treatment method there," Abdul-Hamid said, likely referring to the Islamic medical clinic that had recently opened in the city.

Abdul-Hamid learned to perform hijama himself. He wanted to help people, and it let him earn a living. He did not hide the fact that the treatment provided him with a source of income. He emphasized, however, that he had no set price for the procedure. If a person had no money, he performed the bloodletting for free. Money, he maintained, was not what mattered to him the most. He had been receiving a growing number of requests to "read the Koran over the sick," as the practice of expelling jinns is often called.

"People often end up in the loony bin, they keep them locked up in hospitals, when in fact jinns are the real problem. This method can be used to treat many diseases. Symptoms indicating that a person has been possessed by jinns include chronic headaches, mood swings in the evening, and nervous tension. They prescribe pills that don't help. Everything is written in the Koran. People just don't know about it; they think it's a bunch of nonsense. But this method has been used since the time of the Prophet Muhammad."

Abdul-Hamid spoke of new medical treatments such as hijama and the use of Islamic cosmetics as more than just ways to improve a person's health. These were also "modern" practices imported from Arab countries, ones that he contrasted with the outdated treatments used in Dagestani hospitals. In Abdul-Hamid's view, the solutions described in the Koran were simpler, healthier, and "more natural."

People were turning to Islamic medicine with growing frequency, Abdul-Hamid claimed. It was not just that they were starting to believe in its effectiveness; people either did not trust regular doctors or did not want to pay bribes. Abdul-Hamid recalled the story of a young boy who had been brought to the hospital following an accident. He was unconscious but would survive if he went into surgery immediately. The doctor would not even come down to the emergency room, demanding payment of a specific amount of money before he would even see the patient. The boy was unconscious, had no identification, and there was no way to contact his family. People pleaded with the doctor to save him. When he finally came downstairs, it was too late. The boy had died before the operation even began. It turned out that he was the doctor's son.

When I met Abdul-Hamid a few months later, he announced that he had gotten married again.

"I took a second wife," he said, "a divorcée with a child. In Islam, that's a very good deed. Especially considering there's six women for every man in Russia. If it weren't for Islam, they'd be lonely with no one to fend for them. I'll try to give both the same care. Both of my wives have the same rights. Islam protects them. It's the same with the children. Russian law forbids it, but we're getting an Islamic wedding, and that's the one that really matters," he said.

"Wasn't your first wife upset?" I asked out of curiosity.

"Well . . . she wasn't happy about it. . . . You know how it is."

Before we parted, I told Abdul-Hamid that I would be back in a few months and would be happy to meet with him again.

"Sure, if I'm still here. If I live that long, *inshallah*. Around here, you can never be sure about tomorrow. Only Allah knows."

In Abdul-Hamid's view, sharia was more than just the best possible law; it was also the most "natural" law, one that people needed to follow if they wanted peace and order in their lives. During our conversations, my subject emphasized elements of sharia that provided possible solutions to the problems that plagued Dagestan, including corruption and the failing health care system. Paradoxically enough, my discussion with Abdul-Hamid resembled many other conversations I had had in Dagestan with people in whose lives Islam did not play a significant role. I had heard Abdul-Hamid's story about the doctor's son told several times by a wide range of people. I would often be told about how difficult it was to get anything done without paying a bribe. The only difference was that Abdul-Hamid believed this could be solved with sharia, which, if imposed, could do away with the problem of corruption, nepotism, and so on. Abdul-Hamid wanted to practice his profession and run his store in peace. He wanted to be confident about his future, rather than worry that someone might set fire to his shop for selling "contraband" literature (which happened to his neighbor) or that he or a family member would be arrested.

In a place where people's lives are regulated by violence and *poniatiya*, the idea of creating an Islamic state or imposing sharia is growing increasingly popular. However, it's important to understand these concepts in the local context. For many people like Abdul-Hamid, an "Islamic state" in Dagestan resembles less an abstract textbook caliphate and more a state free of corruption, one governed by clear rules, where people can live and work in peace, where their basic (or as Abdul-Hamid would say, natural) needs are taken care of, and where they do not feel threatened.

Personal practices and narratives of naturalness, natural medicine, and herbal medicine—all widespread in Russian media—mixed with narratives of faith, creating a world in which answers to everyday questions and solutions to mundane problems were found in religion and the practices associated with it. Because they were rooted in people's own stories and the practices of everyday life, personal projects were becoming increasingly popular and with

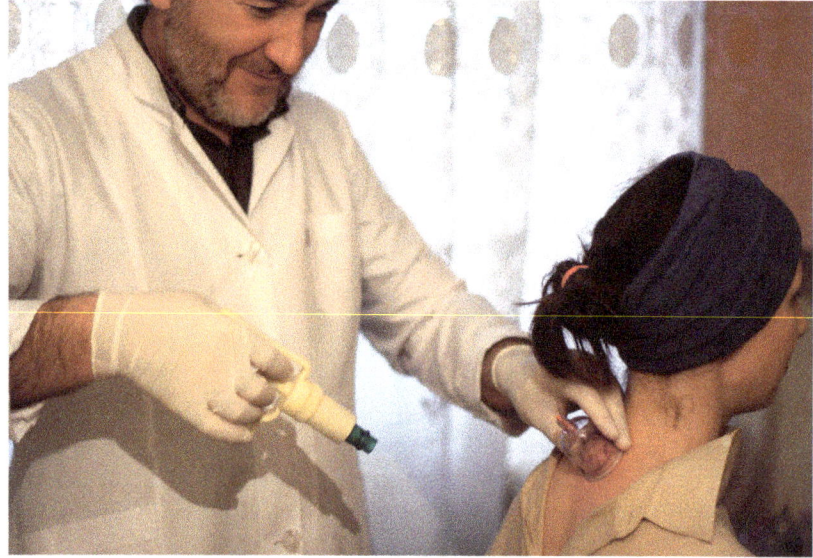

FIGURE 5.3. Medicinal bloodletting procedure (*hijama*). Photo by Iwona Kaliszewska.

them the idea of an Islamic state, which was thought of mainly in contrast to the current "system," its dysfunctional health care system, and corruption.

"We Have to Support Our Jamaat": Community Projects

Alongside projects that called for radical change in all of society or the world, as well as projects that focused on individuals and families, there are noteworthy visions that are primarily concerned with the mountain community or smaller communities located in suburban areas or around mosques. Before I explore in greater detail the local projects premised on maintaining or imposing order in the jamaat, I will briefly review the changes that have taken place in the structure of communities in Dagestan within the past century. This context will elucidate my subjects' statements and actions as well as their ambitions to impose sharia-based order in their villages.

Concern over the continuity of community has a long history in Dagestan. Kinship-territorial communities, known as jamaats, from Arabic, coalesced around the fourteenth and fifteenth centuries. This was a result of the relative political stabilization of the period and the need to organize the use of agricultural land. The issue of defense was likely a significant factor as well.

The kinship-territorial community of the jamaat comprises tukhums (from the Persian word for "family"), each of which trace their lineage back to an actual or fictional ancestor and inhabit a particular area. In Dagestan, even the largest tukhums rarely exceeded the size of a single village. This is notable in that in other republics, extended families (such as the *myssag* in North Ossetia and the *teip* in Chechnya) can be scattered over a larger area. Villagers in Dagestan know their family trees in minute detail and can recall whose ancestors settled a given area the earliest; whether a person belongs to a "better" or "worse" tukhum is also of great importance. Elements of the tukhum system have survived to the present day, particularly the division between noble and common clans, or *uzdeni* (people with full rights) and *lag'aol* (descendants of slaves and captives, typically forbidden from marrying uzdeni). A jamaat typically encompassed a single village but sometimes included outlying settlements (*khutors*). New houses were built one on top of the other, forming a hive-like structure; it is possible that this approach served to reinforce a sense of community. Under the local adats of many jamaats, the sale of land to outsiders was punishable. Land could only be sold with the permission of the other members of the community.

The jamaat structure survived into Soviet times in the form of the kolkhoz. The gradual implementation of the kolkhoz system was relatively successful in Dagestan. Not only did Dagestanis accept the new top-down system; they even adapted it to their traditional way of life. It was not uncommon for a kolkhoz to be led by a person who enjoyed great authority among the villagers, sometimes even the imam. Prayers were held to mark important holidays in the kolkhoz. The kolkhoz did not just operate within the boundaries of a jamaat; it also functioned in a similar manner. The old organizational schemes of the jamaat permeated the structures imposed by the Soviet state. The kolkhoz structure was superimposed over an existing structure.[1]

The marginalization of the region, the processes set off by the collapse of the USSR, the mass migration from villages to cities (which had begun in the USSR, albeit on a much smaller scale), and seasonal migration all threatened the existence of many jamaats, particularly in areas plagued by poverty and unemployment, such as the Tsumadinsky District, whose inhabitants are significantly underrepresented in the republic's government.

The desire to rescue the jamaats and concern about their continued survival became subjects of public debate in many mountain auls. Villagers lamented migration and the dissolution of familial bonds. One solution used in many jamaats was to hold "village days," a festival and holiday that attracted many people who had left a given jamaat. Communities would celebrate other important events such as the construction of a new mosque or school, where they would praise the wealthy donors, many of whom were locals who had migrated to the city but provided financial support to their highland villages and helped their inhabitants find jobs. In some places, these individuals were solely responsible for connecting their village to the natural gas grid, sealing the roads, and renovating and equipping schools and mosques. It was them, and not state institutions, to whom the villagers turned in difficult moments such as the death of a family member or the loss of employment. One of the few influential people of this kind in the Tsumadinsky District was Sagid Murtazaliev, an Olympic champion wrestler and deputy of the People's Assembly of Dagestan. However, not all villages have a "guardian angel," an authority figure with the financial means to support the development of their jamaat.

In the first decade of the twenty-first century, sharia appeared as a new unifying paradigm, one that was relevant not just in view of the desire to review ancestral traditions but more importantly as a means of instilling order and discipline.

Magomed's Story: "Only through Sharia Can We Fight Hypocrisy"

Magomed, aged thirty-four, comes from the village of Kvanada in the Tsumadinsky District (see figure 5.4). We visited him during Ramadan, the Islamic month of fasting. We joined him and his wife on their trip from Agvali to the village, where they were going to prepare for the holiday marking the end of the fast. The end of Ramadan is a period of intense religious practice. During the hours of prayer, the streets are full of men making their way to the mosque (the women pray at home). In Kvanada, the passage of time is marked by daily prayers. It was decided that daylight saving time would not be observed in this region, which meant that in the summer the clocks ran an hour earlier than in the rest of the republic (daylight saving time was abolished in all of Russia in 2011). "That makes it easier to synchronize prayer times," I was told. Appointments are rarely made on the hour in this village. Rather, people will agree to meet "after afternoon prayers" or "after evening prayers." The local shop had stopped selling alcohol and cigarettes a few days earlier.

In the evening, Magomed, the mosque's imam, and a few local authority figures (*avtoritetniye*) climbed a nearby hill to watch for the moon, whose appearance in the sky marked the end of Ramadan. Due to the heavy cloud cover, however, the moon could not be seen. Some villagers, whom Magomed called our Wahhabis, had already broken their fasts: they had called Saudi Arabia

FIGURE 5.4. View of the village Kvanada, Tsumadinsky Region. Photo by Iwona Kaliszewska.

and synchronized their feast with the celebrations taking place in that distant country.

Magomed praised the village's current imam. "He brought order and clear rules," he explained. In Magomed's view, the order and low number of conflicts in the village could only be attributed to the introduction of elements of sharia. When I asked him to name a few, he listed the prohibition of alcohol and cigarettes first, along with mandatory headscarves. "But sometimes they just won't leave us alone," he said, referring, as became apparent during the conversation, to the security forces and the FSB.

My subject compared the current situation to that of the 1990s, when the village split into two factions, each either supporting or opposing Salafi Islam, when families were riven by religious and political divisions and when "brothers killed brothers, when my wife's brother nearly killed me because I wasn't on their side." Magomed hoped that those days would never return. He believed that the village leaders would succeed in maintaining order.

"We all live according to sharia, and we all pray to the same God. We all attend the same mosque, and even if we differ a bit, we try to make everyone comfortable in the village and avoid conflicts," he said.

One night, after evening prayers, we attended an evening meeting.

"This is our jamaat. The most important people in the village," he said, smiling.

The man of the house welcomed us warmly.

"If you don't mind, we'll take this moment before the tea arrives to discuss the matter of the village festival that took place recently. We need to settle everything so that no one feels they have been treated unfairly. And then we'll talk."

The men spoke for while in the local language, Bagvalal, and exchanged bits of paper with notes written on them. When tea was served, they eagerly talked about the festival and praised the organizers and the sponsor—locals who had migrated to the city, some of whom had become wealthy businessmen.

"There were two thousand people—some from as far away as Russia—and not a drop of liquor!" one of the men present said with pride. They invited us to attend the festival the following year. The celebration was not religious in nature: as one of the men present pointed out, there were all kinds of people in attendance, including nonbelievers. The men were especially satisfied with the turnout and were pleased that people had not forgotten their roots and continued to venerate their memory of their ancestors.

Most of the decisions in the village are made by the jamaat, whose members belong to several different tukhums and hold great authority. This group is responsible for making important decisions such as choosing the imam or the head of the administration. The jamaat also rules on whether a particular plot of land may be sold. Soviet authorities created a kolkhoz in Kvanada; private property was confiscated and redistributed by officials. However, the villagers continued to work their ancestral land as they had before, sometimes making "quiet" exchanges with neighbors who had been assigned their plot in the kolkhoz. In many places, plots continued to be inherited informally, and care was taken to ensure that no land was acquired by people outside the community. After the collapse of the USSR, Kvanada returned to its traditional land divisions. A deed from the period of czarist rule and two witnesses were enough to prove ownership to the administration. The villagers successfully lobbied the regional administration to recognize traditional divisions and the above documents. In result, plots of land were legally returned to their former owners.

"There's Yeltsin, then there's Putin, and then who knows who. Why should I have to move to a different piece of land just because of that?" Magomed remarked after a lengthy discussion on the topic of land ownership.

Official elections are only formally held in Kvanada because "what's the point of stirring up trouble?"

"They don't understand; some of them don't even live here on a permanent basis," one of the men said.

"So we get together and talk, and then we decide who gets elected."

With the exception of a few people, none of the villagers are public employees. The head of the administration is formally on the government's payroll but cannot challenge any of the jamaat's decisions and must consult everything with the elders. A policeman from the regional capital makes perfunctory visits on a monthly basis. There is no local law enforcement in the village.

The regional FSB officer (*FSB-shnik*) tries to follow the goings-on in the village through other channels. A few years before our visit, he asked a villager whom he ran into in Agvali, "Any news about the militants? Are they in your village?" The man replied, "They are, and they're staying there as long as this mess continues."

Magomed appreciated how peaceful and orderly the village had been ever since locals "took matters into their own hands." However, he complained that things were not as simple as they seemed, and some people only pretended to obey the rules.

"One time, I walked into a bar because I was looking for a friend and I was told I would find him there. I don't go to such places myself. I walked in, and who do I see but the imam and a few others, all of them pious Muslims, drinking and having fun. They were happy to see me. 'Oh, we're so glad you could join us, Magomed!'"

Magomed himself admitted that despite his best efforts, he did not always succeed in being a good, honest Muslim and living his life according to the Koran. It is not easy, especially for people who work for the government, as he does.

"I know this system and I know how to get around it. I try not to follow the rules of the system [*starayus' etu sistemu nie sobliudat'*]. But a man has to live. . . . I can't get by without a job."

"Anyone who wants to be honest and refuses to steal or take bribes is going to get sacked. They'll just say, 'He's not one of ours' and fire him. One time, a civil servant asked, 'How are we going to work? *Po poniatiyam* [by the criminal code] or *po chelovecheskiy* [like people]?'" Magomed said, explaining that in Dagestan, people had given up on obeying the law long ago and that everyone lived *po poniatiyam*.

"Only sharia can help us fight hypocrisy and all of that," he added.

He did see some improvement, however. He observed that there were more genuinely pious people who honestly fulfilled the commandments of Allah.

I last saw Magomed in 2010. There was a special operation under way in Kvanada, and the village was surrounded by BTRs and other *tekhnika*, as heavy military equipment is known there. I feared that my phone call and my presence might have caused trouble for Magomed, but another acquaintance reassured me that everyone knew one another around there and that no one cared about that.

I was afraid to call Magomed in 2011, not wanting to draw undesired attention to him. I learned from friends that he had taken a second wife and later lost his job. His cousin had been arrested during the raid in Kvanada and later killed.

After returning from Tsumada in 2011, I told a few people in secular Makhachkala about my trip, mentioning the religiosity of the villagers and their problems. I expected them to respond with comments similar to the ones I heard the year before: "So they want a caliphate, do they?," "backward types," and the like. "Proud highlanders" is what I heard from one acquaintance, a man in his early sixties, when I mentioned that Kvanadians "keep the state at bay" and have imposed their own order. I was told a lot about religion and sharia in Kvanada, but there was also the occasional comment about an Islamic state. The idea of the state and its existence were never questioned, nor was there any discussion of the superiority of sharia over secular law. There were frequent references, however, to state officials, representatives of the "system," which the villagers attempted to keep at arm's length in various ways—for instance, by barring policemen from entering the village or by emphasizing that they had no connection to "those people." The jobs held in highest prestige were ones in lowland businesses or in Russia—work which, they said, "offered an honest income." Employment in the public sector (excluding such positions as teachers, for example) was rejected by many as incompatible with the principles of sharia.

"They won't leave me alone." I heard these words repeated by many people in reference to the FSB. The state was not expected to maintain order (although such opinions were voiced as well) as much as it was expected to stay out of the way. The practice of distancing oneself from the state should not be understood to mean, in this case, the practice of nonparticipation, as even individuals who resist the system more or less openly are nevertheless entangled in it. Distancing oneself is instead a moral choice that may or may not involve direct efforts to change the relation of power.

The "Kvanadian project" and many other similar actions and projects I encountered in Dagestan compel us to consider whether, when viewing the state through an anthropological lens, we should concentrate not only on the presence of the state in the lives of people but also on the manner in which the state ceases to serve as the foundation of a person's identity. We might therefore inquire not just how the state is culturally constructed but also how it is deconstructed and what types of power relations are involved in that process.

"Nothing We Do Is Unconstitutional": The Story of Huseyn and Imam of Tindi

We agreed to meet with Huseyn, aged thirty-eight, at dawn, right after morning prayers. "Get up when you hear the muezzin. I'll be there in twenty minutes," he explained. We got in his car and he drove us to his home village. He was pleased that we had chosen to shoot footage for our film in Tindi. Huseyn lived in Makhachkala, but he had grown up in the aul. He drove up the hairpin mountain roads at high speed, hoping to arrive in time for the midday *salat*, the most important of the Friday prayers.

Huseyn became a devout Muslim as an adult; he prayed regularly and made efforts to live according to sharia, even though, as he said, "it's not easy with this system we have." He described himself as "simply Muslim" and did not identify with any particular school. He worked two full-time jobs to support his wife and three children. Huseyn was actively involved in promoting the region: he collected photographs and film footage, wrote about the histories of the auls and compiled biographies of famous locals, posted information about cultural and sporting events, and helped find sponsors among villagers who had left to work in the city. He also made efforts to attract the attention of researchers, historians, and ethnographers by organizing conferences and events.

"I have to be careful because my website is getting pretty popular. It's easy to get in trouble with either side, and both of them want me in their camp. I got in trouble with one side when I mentioned my cousin, a shaykh, in a post about the history of Tsumada. It was just historical information. Now they say I'm on the forest brothers' 'list.' The others are *this* close to labeling my work extremist. I get all sorts of comments on my website, and I can't moderate everything to make sure no one writes anything that's too radical or directed against the state.... People write all sorts of things.... Next thing you know, I'll be accused of separatism," he joked.

Huseyn spoke critically of "the system," but he realized that the situation was very complicated. He knew many people who worked for the government and the police, as well as people who had left the public service "because they couldn't live like that." He did not blame the police or civil servants for the crisis in Dagestan but instead pointed to the system propped up by Moscow—a system he claimed was convenient for businessmen and criminals alike. It was easy to launder money in Dagestan, he said. Nevertheless, Huseyn hoped that things would change for the better: he had been meeting more and more people who tried to live by sharia and refused to take bribes, setting a good example for others. He believed that if there were more people like them, the situation could change.

He told me how problems, including matters of a criminal nature, were typically solved in Dagestan.

"If a person unintentionally kills someone, for example in a car accident, and the police find out, then you pay them money to close the case and stay out of it. You then do a *maslihat*, or reconciliation [*primereniye*]. The elders of the culprit's clan go to the elders of the victim's clan and ask if they would be willing to forgive him and under what conditions. They discuss financial matters. Nowadays, most problems are solved through reconciliation [*po maslihatu*]. Nobody relies on the courts because they're corrupt. Nobody expects any justice from them. You can get any verdict you want—for a bribe. And the police don't mind because they just have less work to do."

"That's right," I said, recalling an event that had happened the previous year. "When a friend of mine had her purse stolen from her apartment and went to the police, they got angry at her for giving them more paperwork to do, and they refused to take the case. They said the thief would never be found anyway."

"Exactly. It can be more difficult with cases of murder or rape, especially if the police find out," Huseyn replied. "Then they [the authorities] demand a lot of money. But there's usually some way to work it out in the end. But if the case goes to trial . . . That's what happened one time in Khasavyurt. Usually when a girl is raped, the family or the victim will drop the charges or change her statement once they reach an agreement on the sum of money to be paid by the rapist. But in this case, the court acquitted the culprits because they were the sons of a government official. They later burned them in the city square. Serves them right."

We arrived in Tindi half an hour before afternoon prayers. The village is located in the mountains, perched over the river Avarskoye Koysu in the Tsumadinsky District (see figure 5.5). Before it was colonized by Russia, this was the most important settlement in the region, one where small jamaats would come together in times of danger. It was a religious center, and many Muslim scholars came from Tindi and nearby Aknada. In the times of Imam Shamil, the village served as a prison for the leader's enemies, earning it the nickname Shamil's Siberia.

Most of Tindi's residents work seasonal jobs in the Rostov Oblast, where they harvest onions. They spend the winter in the aul and go back to the Rostov-on-Don region for the summer, coming home for weddings, funerals, and religious and family celebrations.

Shortly after we arrived, Huseyn went to the mosque for afternoon prayers. He held in his hand a stack of fliers.

"What does it say?" I asked, noting that the fliers were not written in Russian.

"I want to get the residents of the village to put down their nationality as 'Tindi' in the upcoming census."

"Why?"

"The Tindi are a separate nation. Our language is completely different from Avar, and it even has several dialects. We speak Avar, too, because it's used throughout this region. Our children have to learn no fewer than three languages: Russian, Avar, and Tindi. . . . And besides, maybe that way, we could be better represented in the government."

Like other nations belonging to the Andic group, the Tindi were classified as Avar by Soviet linguists, despite the significant lexical and grammatical differences between the two tongues. Avars are strongly represented in local government, which the Tindi believe is unfair, as Huseyn later explained.

Huseyn was an active supporter of the Tindi language and had compiled a list of important Tindi vocabulary words on the website www.tsumada.ru. He also made sure his children spoke his native language. I initially perceived him to be a "national" activist, a person who took up the cause of preserving his language, so I was curious what he thought about the waning popularity of traditional holidays in Tsumada and Dagestan in general.

FIGURE 5.5. View of the village Tindi, Tsumadinsky Region. Photo by Iwona Kaliszewska.

"It's too bad they don't celebrate K'ba [the spring holiday] anymore in Tindi," I said to Huseyn. I was somewhat disappointed: I had traveled to Tindi in the spring in hopes of taking part in the festival. The neighboring region was famed for its grand spring celebrations, replete with masks and colorful costumes. All the old masks in the Tsuntinsky District had been burned a few years earlier, but the celebrations had continued in Tsumada until recently.

"Is it too bad? I don't know about that. It's against Islam," he explained. "Those holidays have pagan roots. In Soviet times, people didn't know what was or wasn't Islam. They thought those rituals were Islamic," he explained. "Now people are starting to learn about Islam and they're putting an end to that stuff."

Huseyn was equally categorical in his statements about fortune-tellers and psychics, whose actions he considered detrimental to society. He argued that they should be forbidden "to purify Islam of paganism."

"You'll stay here for the night," Huseyn said as we pulled up to the house where the imam of Tindi and his wife lived. We sat down at the table, and the imam's wife immediately served tea and went to prepare a meal. The imam, who looked to be about fifty years old, was eager to engage in theological debate. We talked about Christianity and Eastern philosophy. His wife was a homemaker who also gathered herbs and medicinal grasses. There was a power outage during dinner, and the woman lit candles.

The imam talked about the scourge of alcoholism in his village and the domestic violence, arguments, and fighting it caused. Drug addiction was becoming increasingly prevalent among young people (it was not clear whether the imam had all of Dagestan or just Tindi in mind). He said that Islam had helped bring the community together, filling a void and giving their lives meaning. Today, he said, there were only a few villagers who still drank alcohol. Smoking remained an intractable problem: too many older people in the jamaat smoked, but the habit was less common among the youth. Whenever the imam made a decision involving the social life of the community, he would consult it with the jamaat, whose members included representatives of other tukhums, the head of administration, the local policeman, and the imam himself. I learned from Huseyn and other villagers that the imam was the person the residents of Tindi would turn to in the event of a conflict. He resolved disputes by referring to sharia. He talked to couples who wished to get married or divorced, offered advice, and encouraged others to follow the rules of Islam. More than anything else, he wished for peace and harmony in his community. Although the villagers often describe him as "strict," he enjoys significant authority in Tindi.

"Sharia discourages the consumption of alcohol and holding festive weddings with bands and singers," he said.

"And that's why those are all punishable in your village?" I asked.

"Where did you hear that?" the imam asked, somewhat embarrassed. "Well, yes, but it's only a token punishment," he said. "The jamaat decided that these regulations would fight drinking and prevent the corruption of our youth."

I learned of the punishments in May 2008 while drinking vodka with the principal and physics teacher from the local school. The teacher poured the vodka but did not drink any, as he had promised the jamaat that he would quit. Refusing to pour alcohol for a male guest could be seen as a violation of the rules of hospitality. The teachers told us that anyone who drank alcohol in the village had to pay a fine to the imam. They supported the regulation: the punishment was imposed by the imam who, they all agreed, was the most respected person in Tindi.

"Our Islam has nothing to do with extremism," the imam said after a moment. I felt that he was trying to emphasize the peaceful character of the local project. It was possible that he did not entirely trust me and feared that I would get the wrong impression about the use of elements of sharia and punishments in his community.

"There has never been a Wahhabi in this village, and there never will be, *inshallah*," he adds and drops the subject.

I recalled the dusty DVDs sold at the local bazaar, discs with titles like *The True Face of Islam* and *Warning: Extremism!* In 2010, the topic came up much less frequently than it had in 2008. By 2010 and 2011, the villagers were more likely to say, "What Wahhabis? What terrorists? Those are just stories they made up to pull the wool over people's eyes!"

Our conversation about the regulations that had been introduced in the village was not easy; the imam was reluctant to talk about the subject.

"Nothing we do is unconstitutional. We live in a secular country and the law needs to be obeyed," the imam said, emphasizing this point repeatedly over the course of our conversation.

Nor was he eager to discuss the corruption that plagued the republic. "Where *don't* they have corruption?" he responded cagily when I asked him about the problem explicitly.

I did not press the issue. Open criticism of the authorities can have dire consequences, particularly in regions that are underrepresented in the government of Dagestan. As Huseyn later explained, the imam was concerned that his words might be taken out of context. The authorities in Makhachkala already thought of Tsumada as a Wahhabi region.

Whatever his opinion was of the situation at the time, the imam, like many of his generation, spoke warmly of the Soviet period and contrasted it with the present situation.

"The persecution was wrong, but there was plenty that was good. Then they wrecked everything, and how are we supposed to live now?"

He also spoke with pride about the Great Patriotic War in which many Dagestanis fought. He pointed out that there were Tindis among the war heroes. However, he mourned the fact that his compatriots were rewarded for their contributions less generously than the Russians were, despite the former's unquestionable sacrifice for what was, at the time, their homeland.

Like Huseyn and my other subjects, the imam of Tindi held views on Russia, the USSR, and their history that were in line with those shared by other citizens of Russia. It became clear during our conversations that he had a certain admiration for the Soviet modernization project, especially the hydroelectric power stations, factories, and mountain airstrips that it produced. No less important was the feeling of being in the center of things. My interviewees in Tindi recalled, "We really felt like we were part of something. And now . . ." (male, about seventy years old); "We would fly to Transcarpathia, Moscow, Saint Petersburg for holidays—whenever we wanted" (woman, fifty-nine years old). Were these attempts to regulate society through sharia driven by a desire to overcome the republic's peripheralization, which Dagestanis experienced as demodernization?

"We Can Get Young People to Live by the New Rules": Jamilat's Story

Huseyn introduced me to Jamilat, aged fifty, in October 2010, having described her as a charismatic woman known in Tindi for her entrepreneurial skills, her former athletic career in wrestling, and her tumultuous personal life. She ran a general store in the village, which gave her financial independence from her husband. She spent her earnings on building and renovating her children's homes. She received no help from her spouse, who drank and had two other wives and several children.

Jamilat told me about her life, how she had fallen in love with her future husband in school, about wrestling—which she could never pursue professionally despite earning several trophies because "it didn't befit a woman" and her "brother and father wouldn't allow it"—and about her work in the Rostov Oblast, where she and other villagers had harvested onions for the past twenty years or so. She paused for a moment by a photo of the Olympic champion wrestler Sagid Murtazaliev, who had grown up in the region.

"He's a distant relative of mine," she said proudly. I asked if he supported his community in the manner that is common for locals who emigrate to the city: by "finding" jobs for members of the jamaat and funding the construction of schools and mosques. "Yes, he visits once in a while, and we can always count on him in times of trouble."

Jamilat wanted us to meet her parents, who live on a farm a few kilometers outside Tindi. We went to the village administration building to ask her brother to drive us.

"This is my brother's office," she said and ushered us into the room before I could ask what he did. Inside the small office was a Russian and Dagestani flag, black furniture, and a computer. On the wall hung a calendar with a photo of Mecca. I was curious what Jamilat's brother, who was five years her junior, had to say about power relations in the village.

"Who's more important in your village: the imam or the head of administration?" I asked after a brief introductory exchange, curious how he would respond to such a direct question.

"I think the imam is the most important," the young man replied in an amused but somewhat confused tone. "That's the way things work around here. We consult the imam when we make important decisions that affect the community. He's a wise man, and he knows a lot about Islam," he said. "There's also a jamaat in the village, which represents the larger clans. Nothing happens here without their knowledge. That's the system we have here," he added.

We accompany Jamilat and her brother to a modest farm at the bottom of a canyon. Jamilat's mother was busy making dinner. When her father learned that we were shooting a film, he asked where we wanted him to sit and immediately began to tell us the story of his life. Like many older citizens of Russia, he complained about dishonest privatization and fulminated against the government, Boris Yeltsin, and Mikhail Gorbachev.

"Look what they've done to our homeland! They served no one's interests but their own!" the elderly man said, clearly upset about his country's misfortunes. "There's no law, no order, and even the police are involved in corruption. It's a mess. Criminals murder people and buy their way out of jail. The law should be tougher. Say what you will about Stalin, but under his rule the state and the laws were powerful. And then they screwed everything up. Everything's falling apart, the food's no good anymore, and the quality of clothes is terrible. They import everything, there's no natural clothing, it's all chemicals. . . . Russia, Russia . . . We're all one nation. Why do they try to divide us? They pay [workers] more in Moscow than they do here. What sort of country is this?

People are getting kidnapped, murdered. They kidnapped my brother in Chechnya and demanded ten thousand dollars in ransom money. We gave them eight thousand. When he went back to Chechnya a second time and disappeared, no one even called us. There used to be three policemen in the entire district, now there are two hundred. Wherever you go there are cops, prosecutors, detectives, and somehow the law doesn't work. All Putin and Medvedev do is give beautiful speeches. But everything stinks from far away. There's a saying around here: The fish rots from the head. This isn't democracy. Democracy is nothing like this. Thievery is what it is!" He adds, after a moment, "But I live a peaceful life here. Nobody bothers me, lucky for me."

"We're living in tough times: things are messy. There's a war here, a war there," Jamilat said. "Things aren't that bad out here, but in the city, there are shootings, assassinations, and bombings. The mafia, criminals, political scandals, it all comes down from the top. It's about money. If you've got money, you come out on top, and regular people suffer. And the criminals, the explosions? Don't tell me they can't stop that. There was a time when they could, and now they've got all that heavy equipment, anything they need. They say it's the Wahhabis, but we don't know who's behind it. Everyone just points the finger. If there really are militants hiding out in the woods, then why can't they catch them? It's their policy not to. Stalin was capable of deporting all of Chechnya in two days, send them all to Kazakhstan or wherever. And they can't catch a handful of bandits? Anytime something blows up, they conduct raids and arrest innocent people. There were fewer police in the past and fewer problems, too. Russia is the largest country in the world! Don't they have enough land? We work hard, and they get money for nothing. But that's probably how things work everywhere."

Jamilat was a very pious person and was careful not to miss any of the five prayers. She was certain that only strong faith could make a person's deeds good. She wanted everyone in Tindi and Dagestan to follow the teachings of the faith and believed that everything would change then.

"What's most important is to have faith in Allah. He gives you strength, the will to live. If all people had more faith and believed in Allah, our republic, our country, and the whole world would be a different, better place!"

"Do you want to go to a wedding?" Jamilat asked.

"Sure."

"But you know, this is not one of those festive weddings. The imam doesn't allow it. I'll show you the wedding reception I threw last winter," Jamilat said with pride, rummaging through a stack of DVDs. "My oldest son got married. There was music and dance but no alcohol. And I had no control over who came in, whether they were drunk or not. There's always a few people who get drunk. The imam said not to hold receptions at restaurants or banquet halls. Only mawlids are allowed. But it sort of worked out differently: I rented a space and organized a wedding reception. It was peaceful; the guests ate and stayed for a few hours. Everything was calm and polite. Everyone liked it," she recalled, chuckling as she watched the recording. "I set up tables in the school gym and played some music. The imam said, 'One person has this sort of wedding, and next thing you know, there's a second and a third. Islam doesn't permit it. You're not following Islam,' he told me. But I didn't do anything serious. There's always the possibility that a drunk man will come in. But aside from that, everything was fine and decent. . . . I'm not sure if there's anything planned, if there's going to be music or just the mawlid. The imam doesn't forbid us to listen to music at home; we just can't hire a band or hold wedding receptions at restaurants, especially if they serve alcohol. You know how it is: where there's drunk people, there's arguing and fighting. Bad things happen."

"Did you have to pay a fine?" I asked Jamilat.

"A fine? Well, yes. . . . If there's people drinking, you have to pay. I don't encourage people to drink too much. It's a good ban. You can't force old people to change their ways, but we can at least get young people to live by the new rules."

Jamilat flagged down a passing relative, and we all piled into the car. We drove up the mountainside, accompanied by the sound of loud honking and the rapid-fire beats streaming from the speakers. The *lezginka*—the famous fast-paced dance of the highlanders—had already begun on the narrow street in front of the house, with music playing from a car stereo. The house was full of guests when we entered. The bride's father came up and greeted us. The newlyweds were seated in the largest room along with a group of women, while men had gathered in a downstairs room. There was no liquor on the table, but we spotted guests discreetly pouring vodka out of a plastic bottle in the next room. At one point, a pair of cross-dressed guests joined the reception: a woman dressed as a man, and a man dressed as a woman. In the "women's room," the guests began to dance, ignoring the lack of space.

We ducked into the kitchen to rest, and Jamilat proudly listed the many local and traditional wedding customs, dances, and dishes that we simply had to try and talked about the cross-dressers that were an obligatory feature of every wedding reception. She did not know what their presence was supposed to signify. "Maybe to bring luck to the newlyweds?" she wondered. The part of the mustachioed woman dressed in men's clothes was supposed to be performed by a married woman, but there was no such requirement for her male counterpart.[2]

"I remember the weddings in the old days . . . lots of people, fun, and dancing," she recalled. Mawlids[3] are beautiful and Islamic, but when there's no fun or partying, that isn't good either," she concluded.

A few days later, Jamilat met with a few of her friends to prepare a small party for her daughter, who had taken second place in a regional track and field competition. The women gathered in a newly renovated room decorated with wall tapestries bearing Koranic surahs, brought back from Mecca. On large-screen plasma television, the women watched coverage of the K'ba, the spring holiday celebrated during the solstice. Jamilat explained that each year, the holiday was organized by a different tukhum or by anyone willing and able to undertake the task. The holiday was not held that year.

"The imam forbade it," Jamilat said with regret. "He says it's un-Islamic and pagan. Well, I don't know about that. But what do I know?" she added. "Traditions die out with each passing year. I don't think that's good." The women mourned the fact that the holiday was no longer celebrated, but they did not challenge the imam's decision. They had great respect for him and repeatedly emphasized the importance of the rules he had introduced.

"Things used to be merrier," remarked Jamilat's friend Zagra, a woman in her late fifties. Formerly an employee of the public library and a Komsomol activist, Zagra now owned and managed a small business that sewed hijabs and funeral shrouds. Zagra and Jamilat recalled the adventures of their youth, waxing nostalgic not just about their early years but also about their bygone glory. (I heard a similar comment in the village of Urada in the Shamilsky District, where our local host nostalgically recalled the fun and dancing that took place at the club that once stood on the site of the local mosque.) Like many of their peers, Zagra and Jamilat had fond memories of the dances at the local cultural center, the pranks they would play on men, and the masquerades that took place during weddings and the K'ba holiday. Despite their nostalgia for bygone "modernity" and trips to the movies and Moscow, Jamilat and Zagra, like the imam of Tindi, Huseyn, and many other villagers, were dedicated to building a new local order based on Islam, the path they believed to be their best and only response to the crisis they experienced.

My stay in Tindi was coming to an end. I talked to Jamilat as I waited for my ride to Makhachkala. She was somewhat distant and lost in her thoughts. After a moment, I noticed that she kept glancing at the cemetery, where a group of men were digging a grave.

"Did someone die?" I asked, as if it were not obvious.

"Yes," Jamilat replied, still looking at the cemetery.

"A relative of yours?"

"Yes."

A few minutes passed, and she added, "There's a special operation going on in the neighboring district. They killed one of our men. He was serving in OMON, and they sent him [*otpravili v komandirovku*] to the Tsuntinsky District. We'll have to bury him as soon as they bring his body back. That's the custom in our religion."

About fifteen minutes later, Asad, a man in his mid-forties whom Jamilat introduced as her cousin, pulled up to take us to Makhachkala. He spoke with Jamilat in Tindi for a few minutes. Judging from the context and a few specific Russian words used in the conversation, I could tell they were talking about OMON officers who had been killed. We drove off, and I waited for Asad to say more on the subject, but he did not bring it up.

"They say they still haven't been able to get the bodies out. The gunfire hasn't stopped. At least that's what I heard in Agvali. A few others died, too. It's such a shame," Asad said when I asked him directly. "If the higher-ups wanted to, they would scour all of Dagestan in a month. It's a small republic. I once asked an OMON officer about that. He said, 'There are four militants walking through the mountains, and our commanders tell us, "Kill the first and fourth one." Why not all of them? Those are our orders.'"

"Someone benefits from having them around," Asad concluded.

We reached a checkpoint where we were stopped by the police. Asad got out and went into the traffic police building. He was gone for a while, and I was certain he was negotiating a bribe. Some time passed, and a *gaishnik* (traffic policeman) came out to the car. I instinctively pulled out my documents and recalled our go-to alibi for traveling in the region. The gaishnik asked, "You're from Poland, correct?"

"Yes," I replied, expecting a standard interrogation about the purpose of our visit.

"You're lucky you don't live in Russia. But we're proud. We still have a bit of pride left. . . . They won't let us live in peace here in Dagestan. . . . And how are you enjoying Dagestan?" The policeman suddenly changed the subject, as if realizing that he had said too much.

"It's great. It's a very beautiful republic," I replied, still stunned by what he had said and surprised at his lack of suspicion. He had not even checked our papers.

"Safe travels!"

We pulled away from the checkpoint, and Asad recounted his conversation with the gaishnik.

"I asked him why he would pull over 'one of ours.' He said his shift was ending and he needed to write at least one more ticket. He asked me, '*Zem-*

lyak [compatriot], help me out. Let me give you just a hundred-ruble ticket for a broken headlight. I need to write up the protocol [*sostavit' protokol*] to keep the chief off my back.' So I agreed. Let the boy go home. The police chiefs make plenty of money off those simple gaishniks. We understand each other around here, but in Russia, it's a different matter."

We drove out of Avar territory, and Asad fastened his seat belt.

I mulled over my strange conversation with the policeman. I told Asad, who had not been present, about our exchange. It did not surprise him. He replied, calmly, "You see? Even the police have had enough of this. The rank-and-file cops are the ones who usually get killed, and some of them are honest people, too. The police chiefs force them to take bribes and they make a killing off them. There's only so much you can take. Enough is enough [*nastupil perebor*]. Someday, this is all going to change, *inshallah*."

Is Sharia a Remedy for the Collapse of the Jamaats?

The migration to cities in Dagestan and to central and northern Russia has left the mountain jamaats increasingly empty. In many other parts of the Caucasus, such places had already become depopulated in Soviet times, as their inhabitants were resettled or migrated in search of work. Meanwhile, in Dagestan, many of those who had been forcibly removed under Stalin later returned to the mountains, unable to acclimatize to life on the torrid plains.

Today, it's mostly the elderly and mothers with young children who live in the mountains on a permanent basis. Everyone else spends most of the year working in the cities of Dagestan and Russia. Families often have two homes: one on the plains for the winter and another in the mountains for the summer. Despite the significant exodus of people and the seasonal population changes, new roads, mosques, and schools are being built to serve the villages. Efforts of this type, along with the above instances of using sharia to "impose order" on social conditions, may be interpreted as expressions of concern for the community and one's roots. Special celebrations, mosques, madrassas, and schools are often funded by native sons who have achieved financial success. State authorities, when present at all, are only one of many actors, and their influence is diminishing in many places.

My subjects in the highland jamaats admitted that they had gradually grown accustomed to "life without the state." Although they initially hoped for the return of Soviet rule or some sort of replacement, they eventually realized that in financial matters, they had to mainly rely on themselves and their families, relatives, and villagers who have succeeded in the cities.

It is apparent in the life stories shared by my interviewees that "entrepreneurial" efforts, which were often chaotic, frequently involved the entire community, and were sometimes criminal in nature, were gradually replaced with a lifestyle governed by sharia. Life without the state began to be organized according to sharia.

Islamic law is becoming an important paradigm regulating the life of the community, though people interpret it in different ways; they typically stress the order it brings to their village: the curtailment of violence and drunkenness and the increased discipline. Elements of sharia that benefit the community are emphasized: the fight against drug addiction and alcoholism garners much greater support than the ban on festive weddings, celebrations that are suddenly decried as pagan (and that were also considered vital to the life of the community), village festivals, and sporting events. In a sense, the social utility of sharia is regarded as more important than blind adherence to all of its rules, many of which have only recently been learned and have yet to be fully internalized. The introduction of elements of sharia is therefore largely understood as an expression of concern for the jamaat. Perhaps it is also a response to the complaints of its dissatisfied members (such as Jamilat's father and many people of his generation) and their calls for a strong, effective state and laws, "like in Stalin's time."

With hope waning for a top-down order, one derived from the state, civic-minded residents such as Huseyn, the imam of Tindi, and Jamilat have taken to building their own order at the personal level, using sharia as their main point of reference. It is noteworthy that Islamic law is perceived (and presented) by village authorities as compatible with the constitution and legislation of the Russian Federation. Efforts to change the status quo in Dagestan and Russia do not typically involve opposition to the state or its laws. On the contrary, Huseyn wants to increase the Tindis' involvement in the state by defining them as a separate nation; he wants the state to be a pillar of strength, not an obstacle in the lives of his fellow Tindis. For Huseyn, Jamilat, and the imam, sharia is not intended to replace the law of the Russian Federation but rather to balance the chaos of post-Soviet Russia. It is thus a means of instilling order in the life of the community and integrating it—a response to their need to have any order at all.

Conclusion

"So where does their allegiance really lie? With Putin, Stalin, or Islam?" a colleague asked me, somewhat provocatively, after I had attempted to briefly describe my field of research by recounting a few stories from the lives of my interviewees.

As scholars, we often seek unambiguous truths and clear divisions. Meanwhile, my experience researching Dagestan and my attempts to reflect on my own process of acquiring knowledge in the field have helped me understand how we can discover heterogeneous world views without inquiring about them or seeking them out, in situations in which we can easily deconstruct our own constructs and preconceived notions and in which the divisions we use to make sense of certain phenomena are challenged, leaving us in a world replete with ambiguity and uncertainty.

It was not my intent to write about conflict and violence. However, as I followed the lead of my interviewees, I encountered a violence-plagued world far too frequently and directly to simply ignore these experiences. Certain locations—buildings destroyed by special operations, police checkpoints, places patrolled by armed individuals—would trigger in me and in my interlocutors' memories, or even the anticipation, of violence. In this book, I have analyzed how my interviewees experience fear in their daily lives, particularly their fear of torture, a practice that has become a staple of the republic's bureaucratic system.

The state in Dagestan, as I tried to show, is experienced in terms of two opposite aspects: its excess and its absence. In one context, my subjects would describe the hellish experience of torture and talk about the growing number of acquaintances who had been "disappeared"; in another, they were disillusioned and did not count on state officials to maintain their dilapidated roads or plumbing. This simultaneous experience of the absence and excess of the state is a characteristic feature of peripheral areas, where irresponsible authorities care little about the citizens because they need them neither as taxpayers (money comes from the federal budget) nor as voters (results are falsified anyway) and where the only way to exercise authority is violence (Derluguian 2005).

As I attempted to demonstrate, widespread support for Islamic law in Dagestan and "radical" appeals for change in the spirit of Islam should not be interpreted as manifestations of resistance against the state. Rather, they can be seen as attempts to overcome the republic's peripheral status. For the most part, these efforts have been guided by genuine concern for the republic and local communities. Most of the criticism was directed not against the actions of the state but against its inaction at the local level. It follows that the actions and narratives of Dagestani Muslims I describe in this book are not actually religious projects—as I had initially believed—but political projects firmly anchored in the experiences and conceptions of the former USSR and in the contemporary processes of peripheralization and impoverishment.

Although the idea of sharia or an Islamic state might strike terror in the hearts of many people in the so-called West, it is always worth considering the basis of this fear: whether fears are based on evidence and facts and calls for an Islamic state/installment of sharia are a political cover for domination and gross human rights violations, or rather, they are just desperate pursuits of a perceived order and reprieve from violence and injustice. Many Dagestani Muslims believe that in order to create a disciplined and moral society, its members must adhere to the teachings of Islam. This is particularly important in the face of the collapse of the old system and the rejection of the new order, which is perceived in terms of chaos and violence. The practice of distancing oneself from the present and recent past is emphasized by contrasting this period with Islamic "modernity." These actions are driven by a desire to improve the situation in Dagestan, to instill order in reality: the republic, the local community, and often a person's own life; they are attempts to overcome the crisis, mounted by people whose involvement with Islam is, after all, fairly recent. These actions and visions are not uniform. They include not only visions of the state promoted by the USSR but also a concern for one's own jamaat, an attitude rooted in local tradition; they provide guidance for various aspects of people's lives, from law and celebrations to medicine and rules of dress. At times, the proposed actions are at odds with Russian law and may even include calls for violence such as ridding the social space of allegedly harmful people like fortune-tellers and healers.

Aspirations to increase the presence of Islam in the public sphere are encountered in many parts of the world where Muslims reside. Numerous parallels can be drawn between the actions undertaken by the Dagestani faithful and Islamic modernization projects carried out all over the world. Yet, because of the experience of the Soviet period and the post-Soviet era, these local actions display an entirely different character, one rooted in local history and practices. Some similarities may be found here with Central Asia (compare McBrien 2017). The local efforts undertaken by Dagestani Muslims are thus more than just an interesting object of study; on closer examination, they also compel us to consider the generalizations we make and to examine the essentialism these generalizations express with regard to such concepts as "Islam," "sharia law," and "Islamic state." Depending on the context, calls to live according to sharia can signify a desire to live in a state without corruption, a fight against alcohol abuse, or a longing for an all-encompassing ideological project that could integrate a divided society. When a person professes to live according to sharia, he may simply be expressing his conviction that his actions can change not just his own life but also how the community and the republic operate.

Some "new Muslims" describe their aspirations to live according to sharia and to put the idea into practice as not incompatible with the laws of the Russian Federation, and beneficial to the state, society, and the community. On the one hand, new Muslims act out of concern for the republic, their jamaat, or even the state; on the other hand, in terms of social practice, many of these actions—such as criminalizing alcohol consumption, mandating headscarves, or barring the authorities from entering a village—are direct violations of laws grounded in the constitution of the Russian Federation.

My intention in recounting the narratives of Dagestani Muslims and describing their motives is to illustrate a certain paradox. On the one hand, I attempted to demonstrate that the visions of social order espoused by Dagestani Muslims were not manifestations of support for violent extremism. On the other hand, many of their daily actions reinterpreted their concurrent professions of loyalty to, and concern for, the state (compare Yurchak 2006, in reference to the USSR). Many new Muslims genuinely believed in the idea of the state and did not question the need for secular laws or the requirement that these laws be obeyed. Their actions, however, contradicted these claims. Rustam, whose narratives I analyzed in the previous chapter, would likely find common ground with many socialists; like them, he was concerned that he could not identify a goal to which society as a whole could aspire. He therefore

132 CONCLUSION

FIGURE 6.1. Mecca poster and a clock with Putin and Medvedev in a traditional household in Dakhadaevsky District. Photo by Iwona Kaliszewska.

adhered to the norms of sharia in his own life and wanted all residents of Dagestan to do likewise, regardless of whether these religious principles were compatible with federal law. The imam of Tindi and a number of other imams that I talked to stressed that the norms of sharia implemented in their villages were compatible with the constitution, while issuing fines for offenses that were not punishable under Russian law. The actions of these individuals were not motivated by resistance, yet they did not align, as it were, with the message they directed to the members of their communities and to me.

During the course of my research, statements of loyalty to the state were gradually becoming little more than a form (as Yurchak observed of the final years of the USSR), one identified and shared by others and reproduced during the commemoration of the victory in the Great Patriotic War. This form, however, became increasingly detached from actual practice. Russian laws were violated as a matter of course; they were perceived to be vague, byzantine, and intentionally written to create opportunities for corrupt behavior on the part of public officials. From this perspective, sharia-motivated actions that violate the laws of the Russian Federation were, on the one hand, no different from the practice of following one's "own law," observed by many scholars of Russia in the 1990s (e.g., Humphrey 2018; Ledeneva 1998, 2014). On the other hand, own laws (*svoi zakony*) were often local in scope and sometimes criminal in nature and were unlikely to have been considered as proj-

CONCLUSION 133

FIGURE 6.2. Men gather to dig a grave for a policeman shot dead during a counterterrorism operation in the mountains. Photo by Iwona Kaliszewska.

ects that could encompass all of Russia or a particular region of the country. Meanwhile, the actions undertaken by Dagestani Muslims to introduce sharia were usually "positive projects"; they contained proposals for new rules and legal principles and were inscribed into a broader pan-Islamic context.

Although it is difficult to formulate specific forecasts, we may venture the hypothesis that in the lives of everyday Dagestanis, the state will increasingly become nothing more than an empty form, one decorated with Russian flags and pictures of Putin, and reproduced through statements of loyalty to the authorities, expressed through support at the ballot box. Inside, this form is slowly being filled by sharia, the main paradigm regulating the everyday lives of a growing number of the republic's residents, including many local officials, policemen, OMON officers, and even some employees of the FSB.

Epilogue

The analysis presented in this book refers mostly to the turbulent period preceding numerous departures for ISIS. Almost all of my interviewees knew someone who left for ISIS in the years that followed—people who decided to build their futures in the Islamic State. We will never learn what their real motivations were. Were they lured by local or online recruiters or by their peers? From what I have gathered from family members and the "wives" who returned, many of those who left claimed to "have had enough": enough of the rampant injustice, state violence, constant persecutions, and arrests. Enough of living in constant fear that most of my subjects learned to endure. Other families, however, were puzzled by their relatives' decisions and recalled the ISIS fighters in their as not having been particularly pious, with little religious knowledge, and no association with the so called bearded friends so feared by their parents. They were not unemployed or otherwise financially excluded; some had government jobs—one even worked as a policeman—while others have parents who secured or bought them a public sector job with a stable and decent income, sufficient to support a family. Most of them were in their twenties or early thirties. They belonged to a generation that had not experienced life in the Soviet Union, a generation brought up by either nonreligious parents or parents who had only recently turned to Islam, like most of the individuals in this book.

They left unexpectedly, unhindered by the security forces that were otherwise all too quick to act and catch actual or alleged terrorists. A relative of one of my informants went through great pains to compel authorities to prevent her newlywed granddaughter and her husband, both in their early twenties, from leaving to join the Islamic State. She succeeded only after reaching out to her former classmate, a man who had worked for the FSB in the 1990s and maintained ties with his younger colleagues. The would-be ISIS supporter was put in jail for a year and she was left in peace. "Your jihad is over," her grandmother told her. "Now you go and get a job." Other young couples were not as lucky; by the time their families had learned of their departure, it was often too late to stop them. They claimed to be going to Turkey on business or vacation. Most of the men I heard about were killed; a few stayed in the region or fled to Ukraine. Those whose families had sufficient financial resources and connections managed to bring the women and children back from Syria or Iraq and then secure a new life for them with forged documents and a new identity, or otherwise make sure they would be left in peace by the FSB. Poorer or otherwise insecure families, however, did not have the means to help them or feared persecutions from members of the family or tukhum. Other ISIS survivors had no one to ask for help. I do not know if Aishat, whose story I described in the prologue, or her sisters and brothers in faith joined ISIS. I lost touch with her, as I did with many of the people I met in the course of my research.

Acknowledgments

I am indebted above all to my Dagestani friends who offered me their time and insight into their lives. They include Abdurakhman Yunusov, Gurizada Kamalova, Elena Sepikhanova, Tania and the late Efendi Chutuev, Elmira Kurbanova, Irina, Aleksander, Anya and Abutrab Aliverdiev, Gusein Halilulaev, Dmitry, Aleksander and Natasha Krishtopa, Shamil Shikhaliev, and the residents of Tindi, in particular Jamilat who was the main protagonist of the documentary *The Strongwoman* (dir. Kacper Czubak and Iwona Kaliszewska, Studio Munka 2013). I owe my warmest thanks to many other people I met on my way who prefer to remain anonymous or whose name I did not have a chance to ask. I also owe my warmest thanks to my co-researchers who accompanied me to Dagestan at different stages of the fieldwork, in particular Karolina Rzemieniuk, Maciej Falkowski, Ieva Raubisko, and Iwa Kołodziejska.

I would like to extend gratitude to Georgi Derluguian of New York University in Abu Dhabi and Bruce Grant of New York University for their detailed and encouraging reviews, which helped me to improve the manuscript.

This book went through many revisions. It had many critical readers who helped me to improve the manuscript. They include my colleagues from the Institute of Ethnology and Cultural Anthropology at the University of Warsaw: Lech Mróz, Renata Hryciuk, Iwa Kołodziejska, Helena Patzer, and Karolina Bielenin-Lenczowska, as well as my friends Magdalena Lejman, Aneta Strzemżalska, Ieva Raubisko, Ekaterina Kapustina, and Asmaa Donahue.

I extend my thanks for the generous funding from the Kościuszko Foundation in 2012, which allowed me to work on the manuscript and conduct library research while at IERES at George Washington University. My stay at UC Berkeley between 2014 and 2016, funded in part by the Volkswagen Foundation, helped me immensely to improve the first and second version of the book. More recent updates, between 2016 and 2021, were possible thanks to a grant from the National Center for Science in Poland, research grant number 2015/19/D/HS3/02362. I also gratefully acknowledge the support of the Institute of

Ethnology and Cultural Anthropology and the flexible teaching schedules that allowed me to spend more time in the field.

My very special appreciation and thanks are owed to my brilliant translator, Arthur Barys. Without his professional language skills and great cultural knowledge of the region, the publication of this book would not have been possible. He deserves special thanks not only for his translation but also for his painstaking work in compiling and checking the list of references and other minutiae—tasks that, for the sake of the reader and my family, I did not carry out on my own.

Finally, I reserve my greatest thanks for my husband, Sebastian Kaliszewski, for his comments on the very early and very late versions of the manuscript, and for my family members for their patience in the face of my continuing need to work when I should have been spending time with them.

All of our reviewers and friends have helped me to improve the manuscript, but any mistakes contained herein are solely my own.

Notes

Prologue

1. The names of my informants have been changed to protect their identities.
2. Mawlids gained popularity in the 1960s and '70s because they did not require mosques, which were, for the most part, closed in Soviet times. Since the date of the prophet's birthday is unknown, mawlids were celebrated on various occasions, taking the place of other forms of religious practice forbidden in the USSR.
3. At the time of this conversation, Mukhu Aliyev was no longer the president of Dagestan, having served from 2006 to 2010.
4. *Salvadora persica*, or the toothbrush tree.

Introduction

1. I wish to thank Ieva Raubisko for this observation.
2. For a more detailed discussion of the political transformations in Dagestan, see chapter 1.
3. Kacper Czubak, Maciej Krupa, and I.
4. In response to postmodern doubts about the purpose of descriptive ethnography and associated concerns about anthropologists' entanglement in colonial power relations, Scheper-Hughes postulates the practice of a "good enough" ethnography.

1. Political and Social Instability in Dagestan

1. *Zakat*: One of the five pillars of Islam. A form of obligatory alms paid to the poor, calculated based on one's income and possessions (usually 2.5 percent, or 1/40) above a certain threshold.
2. See, for example, https://www.kavkaz-uzel.eu/articles/198813/.
3. No official evidence exists of such connections, but experts have expressed such opinions in private conversations.
4. The Russian Empire built fortresses and settled Cossacks in the Caucasus and provided financial support to the local aristocracy, whose status was nevertheless completely different from that of their Russian counterparts. The free highlanders of Dagestan and the Russian serfs also differed in terms of their social status. The sociopolitical system forcefully imposed on the region never fully took root, which was one of the reasons for the Russo-Caucasian War, a conflict that ended in the defeat of the Dagestani highlanders in 1856.

5. During the Russian Revolution, Dagestani highlanders largely sided with the Bolsheviks, who broke with their predecessors' strategy of government: instead of conquering Dagestan by force, they promised the highlanders autonomy, sharia, and the right to elect local officials according to local custom. Communism was touted as "compatible" with sharia. Sharia courts continued to operate in Dagestan in the early years of the new state, but this ended in the late 1920s when Muslim clerics and scholars became the targets of a campaign of mass persecution.

6. Jamaat, from the Arabic word meaning "assembly" or "community." The term is used in several meanings in the Caucasus. It typically refers to a community based on shared territory (a single village can be a jamaat) or ideology (such as a jamaat formed around a Salafist leader). A jamaat can also be a general assembly in which a community makes common decisions about its social and religious life (Falkowski and Marszewski 2010, 235).

7. The Khasavyurt Accord, signed in 1996, recognized Chechnya as de facto independent state. However, the republic's short period of self-rule ended in chaos and soaring crime rates (which can likely be attributed in part to the meddling of the Russian security services).

8. In 2004, for example, the Kremlin decided that regional governors would be appointed, not elected, thereby decreasing the citizens' already low involvement in politics.

9. Like many other constituents of the Russian Federation, Dagestan relies heavily on subsidies from the federal budget. See, for example, Matveeva and Savin (2012).

10. Naturally, these were not the only reasons for the Russian exodus. This process was also spurred by instability in Dagestan, particularly the activity of criminal groups, which would target individuals who lacked extensive networks of influential relatives—as was the case with most Russians—and pressure them into selling their apartments at low prices.

11. http://krizis-kopilka.ru/archives/49104; https://vestikamaza.ru/news/mirovye-novosti/nazvany-samye-bednye-regiony-rossii/; http://kavpolit.com/articles/o_sostojanii_ekonomiki_respubliki_dagestan_za_2013-32113/; https://www.pravda.ru/news/economics/1359078-zarplata/.

12. Dagmara Maslova (2019) estimates that half of Dagestan's gross domestic product comes from shadow income.

2. Torture, Exorcisms, and Checkpoints

1. From Abrams's (1988) "Notes on the Difficulty of Studying the State."

2. http://www.memo.ru (accessed regularly since 2007).

3. Roughly equivalent to the highway patrol in the United States. GAI falls under the Ministry of Internal Affairs and is tasked with maintaining the security of roads.

4. UAZ 496, a vehicle commonly used in operations conducted by the Soviet and Russian military.

5. In 2010, I conducted fieldwork with Ieva Raubisko of Oxford University.

6. I discuss the bureaucratic dimension of torture in greater detail in an article about the Dagestani experience of the state (Kaliszewska 2015) published in the volume *State and Legal Practice in the Caucasus* (Voell and Kaliszewska 2015). The article is also based on part of the fieldwork used in this book.

7. As Benjamin famously writes in his essay "The Critique of Violence": "The law's interest in a monopoly of violence vis-à-vis individuals is not explained by the intention of preserving legal ends but, rather, by that of preserving law itself; that violence, when not in the hands of the law, threatens it not by the ends that it may pursue but by its mere existence outside the law" (1996, 1:239).

8. A good depiction of these processes can be found in Weissberg-Cybulski (1952).

9. The exorcisms were recorded on camera. Abdul-Hamid tried to explain to us (accompanying me were Kacper Czubak and Maciej Krupa) what was happening during the course of the ritual.

10. *Yedinobozhniki*: believers in one god.

11. I refer to this voice as the jinn in the remainder of this chapter.

12. A neighborhood in Makhachkala that is home to an Orthodox church.

13. This excerpt is incomprehensible, but the speaker mentions the future coming of Jesus.

14. Abdul-Hamid uses the word *boruyeshsya* rather than the correct conjugation, *boroshsya*.

15. Arabic: *Masha'Allah*, "God has willed it," a phrase used to express approval or joy.

16. Why would Igor, who self-identifies as Christian, use *yedinobozhniki* as an epithet against others? Was it because Salafi-oriented Muslims use the term to differentiate themselves from members of Sufi brotherhoods (whom they do not regard as true monotheists), without considering the existence of other monotheists such as Christians? I owe this question to Bruce Grant of New York University.

17. I conducted part of my fieldwork in March 2010 with Iwa Kołodziejska.

18. The text of the law is available at http://www.fas.org/irp/world/russia/docs/law_980725.htm.

19. Checkpoints served a somewhat similar function in the USSR: policemen paid higher prices to be assigned to roadblocks on more profitable routes—for example, ones leading to resorts—which meant that passing drivers were forced to pay higher bribes (unless they shared family or clan ties with the police officer or came from the same village or region) (King 2008, 178).

20. Helga Tawil-Souri (2017) adds "time" dimension to the haunting experience inside the checkpoint." She argues that checkpoints point to Israel's colonial practice of controlling and erasing Palestinian time. In Dagestan, "Call me when you pass the checkpoint" is a frequently used phrase, one that points to another temporality: it is only after one passes the checkpoint that time begins to flow in a secure and predictable way.

3. The Resurgent Importance of Islam in the Everyday Lives of Dagestanis

1. In the same period, Azerbaijan witnessed a rise in the popularity of Turkish names and ones inspired by classic epic literature, rather than Muslim names.

2. This raises a question: Did Gorbachev's *sukhoy zakon* (dry law) encourage Islamization, and if so, to what extent? Did it lend credibility to the liberalization campaign? (I wish to thank Lech Mróz for bringing these questions to my attention.)

3. Detailed data on ethnic groups and their classification by Soviet linguists are available at www.kaukaz.net in the section titled "Nations of the Caucasus."

4. Although national activism in all its forms was actively suppressed under the Soviet Union, each citizen was assigned a particular nationality that was inscribed in his or her internal passport. Rogers Brubaker (1996) argues that this practice strengthened people's ties with the groups to which they nominally belonged.

5. A detailed description of the political system of Dagestan in the 1990s can be found in Robert Ware and Kisriev (2009).

6. Although the answer is a topic for a separate discussion, the obvious question to ask here is: To what extent did the effectiveness of the Soviet policy of dominance contribute to the establishment of Russian as the lingua franca of Dagestan?

7. In the fall of 1999, units led by Shamil Basayev and Ibn al-Khattab, and supported by radical militants from Dagestan, attacked the Tsumadinsky and Botlikhsky Districts, with the expectation that local residents would join their fight for a free and Islamic Dagestan and Chechnya. This did not occur. Seeing the incursion by Chechen-Dagestani forces as an act of aggression, Dagestanis responded with fierce resistance, holding the attackers at bay until the arrival of federal troops, who routed Basayev and Khattab's units and attacked other so-called Islamic enclaves in Dagestan (among them Karamakhi and Chabanmakhi).

8. Efforts by intellectual circles in Moscow prevented the implementation of this law at the federal level, but the bill was passed in Karachay-Cherkessia and Ingushetia (based on conversations with Alexei Malashenko in March 2012 in Washington, DC).

9. The exact number of orders is impossible to determine, as there are no statistics or data collected on this topic, and many orders practice their faith privately or even underground. The data provided here come from my conversations with analysts and researchers who specialize in the processes taking place in the region but who are not necessarily experts on religious transformations.

10. For further discussion, see, for example Shikhaliyev (2006).

11. Tariqa, "path," a term used in Sufism to describe the path that is followed by members of a Sufi order.

12. This paragraph is adapted from an unfinished and unpublished article I cowrote with Maciej Falkowski in 2009.

13. *Jamaat Shariat*: in simple terms, a group that unites individuals fighting the secular authorities under Islamic banners.

14. Approximate date. The reorganization of underground groups occurred earlier, and in 2009, after a multiyear hiatus, there was a resurgence of attacks (including suicide attacks) and bombings on the streets of the North Caucasus.

4. Wahhabis, Tariqatists, and "New Muslims"

1. *Madhhab*, an Arabic word meaning "school of law." There are four schools of law in Sunni Islam: Hanafi, Maliki, Hanbali, and the most popular madhhab in Dagestan, Shafi'i.

2. Russian *tarikatysty*, from *tariqa*, "path," a term used in Sufism to describe the path that is followed by members of a Sufi order.

3. From the Russian acronym DUMD, Dukhovnoe Upravlyenye Musulman Dagestana, the Spiritual Board of Muslims of Dagestan (muftiyat).

4. During my research, particularly after 2009, I encountered this term being used to convey a different meaning, one akin to "nonpracticing Muslim" or even "an impostor pretending to be a Muslim" or "false Muslim."

5. Ahlu Sunna, a "peaceful Salafi" religious movement founded in 2010 by Abbas Kebedov. The movement is becoming increasingly popular in Dagestan, though I cannot estimate the size of its membership.

6. Whether the term *revival* or *revivals* can be used in reference to ethnic and national processes in Dagestan remains a subject of debate. The Russian term used to describe these processes is *natsionalniye dvizheniya*. Cognizant of the nuances involved in translating the word *natsionalniy*, I have chosen to use the phrase *national revival*.

7. *Ziyara*, from the Arabic "to visit": a pilgrimage or place of pilgrimage.

8. The birthday of the prophet falls in the third month of the Islamic calendar. In Dagestan, the word *mawlid* also means a prayer said at a wedding, following the birth of a child, or at a cemetery. This term is sometimes used interchangeably with the word *dhikr*.

9. A term commonly used to denote armed law enforcement officers, the military, and members of other special units that target alleged terrorists.

10. Islamic songs with lyrics centered on religious themes.

11. Literally *Star Factory*, a Russian television talent show similar to *American Idol*.

12. At this stage of my research (spring 2008), I was accompanied by Maciej Falkowski of the Center for Eastern Studies in Warsaw.

5. Sharia

1. For more, see Bobrovnikov (2020).

2. In the neighboring region of Tsumta, Yurii Karpov and Ekaterina Kapustina witnessed locals donning wolf and bear masks; Kapustina also reports instances of cross-dressing at weddings (from a private conversation with Ekaterina Kapustina, October 2021).

3. Here, a wedding organized without music or alcohol, where collective prayer is performed by a group of invited men.

References

Abrams, Philip. 1988. "Notes on the Difficulty of Studying the State." *Journal of Historical Sociology* 1(1): 58–89.
Aretxaga, Begoña. 2003. "Maddening States." *Annual Review of Anthropology* 32(1): 393–410.
Babich, Irina, and Akhmet A. Yarlykapov. 2003. "Kabardino-Balkariya: Tendentsii razvitiya i problemy overmining islamskogo dvizheniya." *Tsentral'naya Aziya i Kavkaz*, no. 4: 189–200.
Benjamin, Walter. 1968. "Theses on the Philosophy of History." In *Illuminations: Essays and Reflections*, edited by Hannah Arendt, translated by Henry Zohn. New York: Schocken Books.
———. 1996. *Selected Writings: 1913–1926*. Vol. 1. Cambridge, MA: Harvard University Press.
Bobrovnikov, Vladimir. 2020. "Withering Heights: The Re-Islamisation of a Kolkhoz Village in Dagestan: A Micro-history." In *Allah's Kolkhozes: Migration, De-Stalinisation, Privatisation, and the New Muslim Congregations in the Soviet Realm (1950s–2000s)*, edited by Christian Noack and Stephane A. Dudoignon, 367–97. Berlin: De Gruyter.
Bobrovnikov, Vladimir, Florian Muelfried, and Sergey Sokolovskiy. 2011. "From Collective Farm to Islamic Museum? Deconstructing the Narrative of Highlander Traditions in Dagestan." In *Exploring the Edge of Empire: Socialist Era Anthropology in the Caucasus and Central Asia*, 99–117. Reihe, Germany: Halle Studies in the Anthropology of Eurasia.
Boddy, Janice. 1994. "Spirit Possession Revisited: Beyond Instrumentality." *Annual Review of Anthropology* 23(1): 407–34.
Brubaker, Rogers. 1996. *Nationalism Reframed: Nationhood and the National Question in the New Europe*. Cambridge: Cambridge University Press.
Comaroff, Jean, and John Comaroff, eds. 2008. *Law and Disorder in the Postcolony*. Chicago: University of Chicago Press.
Derluguian, Georgi. 2001. "The Forgotten Complexities of the North Caucasus Jihad." In *Caucasus Paradigms: Anthropologies, Histories and the Making of the World Area*, edited by Bruce Grant and Lale Yalçın-Heckmann, 1–24. Berlin: LIT Verlag.
———. 2005. *Bourdieu's Secret Admirer in the Caucasus: A World-System Biography*. Chicago: University of Chicago Press.
Eckert, Julia. 2005. "The 'Trimurti' of the State: State Violence and the Promises of Order and Destruction." *Max Planck Institute for Social Anthropology Working Papers*, no. 80: 181–217.

Edwards, David B. 2012. "Afghanistan, Ethnography, and the New World Order." In *Ethnographic Fieldwork: An Anthropological Reader*, edited by Antonius C. G. M. Robben and Jeffrey A. Sluka, 387–98. Hoboken, NJ: Wiley-Blackwell.

Evans, Brad. 2020. "Why We Should All Read Walter Benjamin Today: Brad Evans in Conversation with James Martel." *Los Angeles Review of Books*, February 3, 2020. https://www.lareviewofbooks.org/article/histories-of-violence-why-we-should-all-read-walter-benjamin-today/.

Falkowski, Maciej, and Mariusz Marszewski. 2010. "The 'Tribal Areas' of the Caucasus: The North Caucasus—an Enclave of 'Alien Civilization' within the Russian Federation." *Prace OSW*, no. 30. https://www.osw.waw.pl/sites/default/files/prace_34_0.pdf.

Gammer, Moshe. 1994. "The Beginnings of the Naqshbandiyya in Dāghestān and the Russian Conquest of the Caucasus." *Die Welt des Islams* 34(2): 204–17.

———. 2002a. "Shamil and the Murid Movement, 1830–1859: An Attempt at a Comprehensive Bibliography." *Central Asian Survey* 21(3): 333–40.

———. 2002b. "Walking the Tightrope between Nationalism(s) and Islam(s): The Case of Daghestan." *Central Asian Survey* 21(2): 133–42.

———. 2005. "Between Mecca and Moscow: Islam, Politics and Political Islam in Chechnya and Daghestan." *Middle Eastern Studies* 41(6): 833–48.

Green, Linda. 1999. *Fear as a Way of Life: Mayan Widows in Rural Guatemala*. New York: Columbia University Press.

Hallaq, Wael B. 1999. "The Authenticity of Prophetic Ḥadîth: A Pseudo-problem." *Studia Islamica*, no. 89: 75–90.

Hebdige, Dick. 1979. *Subculture: The Meaning of Style*. London: Methuen.

Herzfeld, Michael. 2016. *Cultural Intimacy: Social Poetics and the Real Life of States, Societies, and Institutions*. London: Taylor & Francis.

Humphrey, Caroline. 2018. *The Unmaking of Soviet Life: Everyday Economies after Socialism*. Ithaca, NY: Cornell University Press.

Huntington, Samuel. 2007. "The Clash of Civilizations Revisited." *New Perspectives Quarterly* 24(1): 53–59.

Jeganathan, Pradeep. 2004. "Checkpoint: Anthropology, Identity, and the State." In *Anthropology in the Margins of the State*, edited by Veena Das and Deborah Poole, 67–80. Santa Fe, NM: James Curry.

Kaliszewska, Iwona. 2015. "Daghestani Experiences of the State." In *State and Legal Practice in the Caucasus*, edited by Stéphane Voell and Iwona Kaliszewska, 113–33. Farnham, UK: Ashgate.

———. 2020. "Halal Landscapes of Dagestani Entrepreneurs in Makhachkala." *Ethnicities* 20(4): 708–30. https://doi.org/10.1177/1468796820905692.

Kaliszewska, Iwona, and Jagoda Schmidt. 2022. "'Nobody Will Marry You If You Don't Have a Pension.' Female Bribing Practices in Dagestan, North Caucasus." *Caucasus Survey* 10(1): 1–24.

Karpov, Yuriy Y., and Ekaterina Kapustina. 2011. *Gortsy posle gor: Migratsionnyye protsessy v Dagestane v XX—nachale XXI veka, ikh sotsial'nyye i etnokul'turnyye posledstviya i perspektivy*. St. Petersburg, Russia: Peterburgskoye Vostokovedeniye.

Kemper, Michael. 2002. "Khālidiyya Networks in Daghestan and the Question of Jihād." *Die Welt des Islams* 42(1): 41–71.

King, Charles. 2008. *The Ghost of Freedom: A History of the Caucasus*. Oxford: Oxford University Press.

Knysh, Alexander. 2007. "Contextualizing the Salafi-Sufi Conflict (from the Northern Caucasus to Hadramawt)." *Middle Eastern Studies* 43(4): 503–30.

Kvedaravičius, Mantas. 2008. "Dreaming Conspiracies: Experiencing the Law in Post-Soviet Chechnya." Paper presented at the EASA "Experiencing Diversity and Mutuality" conference, Ljubljana, August 26–29.

Lambek, Michael. 1981. *Human Spirits: A Cultural Account of Trance in Mayotte*. Cambridge: Cambridge University Press.

———. 1993. *Knowledge and Practice in Mayotte: Local Discourses of Islam, Sorcery and Spirit Possession*. Toronto: University of Toronto Press.

Ledeneva, Alena V. 1998. *Russia's Economy of Favours: Blat, Networking and Informal Exchange*. Cambridge: Cambridge University Press.

———. 2014. *How Russia Really Works: The Informal Practices That Shaped Post-Soviet Politics and Business*. Ithaca, NY: Cornell University Press.

Lewis, Bernard. 2004. *The Crisis of Islam: Holy War and Unholy Terror*. New York: Random House.

Malashenko, Alexey. 2001. *Islamskiye oriyentiry Severnogo Kavkaza*. Moscow: Moscow Carnegie Center.

Marranci, Gabriele. 2020. *The Anthropology of Islam*. London: Berg.

Maslova, Dagmara. 2019. *Budget and Tax Instruments of Economic Policy and Socioeconomic Dynamics of the Regions of the European Part of Russia (2000–2014)*. Pyatigorsk, Russia: PGU.

Matveeva, Anna, and Igor Savin. 2012. *North Caucasus: Views from Within. People's Perspectives on Peace and Security*. London: Saferworld. https://www.saferworld.org.uk/downloads/pubdocs/North%20Caucasus%20PPP%20English%20revised.pdf.

McBrien, Julie. 2017. *From Belonging to Belief: Modern Secularisms and the Construction of Religion in Kyrgyzstan*. Pittsburgh, PA: University of Pittsburgh Press.

Navaro-Yashin, Yael. 2002. *Faces of the State: Secularism and Public Life in Turkey*. Princeton, NJ: Princeton University Press.

Nguyen, Vinh-Kim, and Karine Peschard. 2003. "Anthropology, Inequality, and Disease: A Review." *Annual Review of Anthropology* 32(1): 447–74.

Omelchenko, Elena, Hilary Pilkington, and Gusel Sabirowa. 2002. "Islam in Multi-ethnic Society—Identity and Politics." In *Islam in Post-Soviet Russia: Public and Private Faces*, edited by Hilary Pilkington and Galina Yemelianova, 210–241. New York: Routledge.

Orttung, Robert, and Sufian Zhemukhov. 2017. *Putin's Olympics: The Sochi Games and the Evolution of Twenty-First Century Russia*. London: Routledge.

Pelkmans, Mathijs. 2011. *Defending the Border: Identity, Religion, and Modernity in the Republic of Georgia*. Ithaca, NY: Cornell University Press.

Pilkington, Hilary, and Galina Yemelianova. 2003. "Official and Unofficial Islam." In *Islam in Post-Soviet Russia: Public and Private Faces*, edited by Hilary Pilkington and Galina Yemelianova, 117–63. New York: Routledge.

Poole, Deborah. 2004. "Between Threat and Guarantee: Justice and Community in the Margins of the Peruvian State." In *Anthropology in the Margins of the State*, edited by Veena Das and Deborah Poole, 35–66. Santa Fe, NM: James Curry.

Pytko, Aleksandra. 2008. "'I'm Not Sick, I Just Have Pain': Silence and (Under) communication of Illness in a Nicaraguan Village." Paper presented at the First Global Conference: The Patient, Salzburg, July 11.

Raubisko, Ieva. 2009. "Proper 'Traditional' versus Dangerous 'New': Religious Ideology and Idiosyncratic Islamic Practices in Post-Soviet Chechnya." *Journal of the Anthropological Society of Oxford* 1(1): 70–93.

———. 2012. "Life in a Negative-Positive Space: Moral Transformations in Post-war Chechnya." PhD thesis, University of Oxford.

Rohoziński, Jerzy. 2005. *Święci, Biczownicy i Czerwoni Chanowie: Przemiany Religijności Muzułmańskiej w Radzieckim i Poradzieckim Azerbejdżanie*. Monografie Fundacji Na Rzecz Nauki Polskiej. Wrocław, Poland: Wydawnictwo Uniwersytetu Wrocławskiego.

Scheper-Hughes, Nancy. 1995. "The Primacy of the Ethical: Propositions for a Militant Anthropology." *Current Anthropology* 36(3): 409–40.

Scheper-Hughes, Nancy, and Margaret M. Lock. 1987. "The Mindful Body: A Prolegomenon to Future Work in Medical Anthropology." *Medical Anthropology Quarterly* 1(1): 6–41.

Scott, James C. 1998. *Seeing like a State: How Certain Schemes to Improve the Human Condition Have Failed*. New Haven, CT: Yale University Press.

Shikhaliyev, Shamil'. 2006. "Sufiyskiy sheykh segodnya." *Etnograficheskoye obozreniye*, no. 2: 24–32.

Shikhsaidov, Amri. 1999. "Islam v Dagestane." *Tsentral'naya Aziya i Kavkaz* 4(5).

Smith, Wilfred Cantwell. 1991. *The Meaning and End of Religion*. Minneapolis, MN: Fortress Press.

Solonenko, Mikhail, and Yuriy Karpov. 2011. "'Silovoy resurs' vo vnutrenney politike Dagestana." In *Radlovskiy sbornik*, edited by Y. K. Chistov and M. A. Rubtsova, 118–32. Sankt Petersburg: Rossiyskaya Akademiya Nauk, Muzey Antropologii i Etnografii.

Taussig, Michael T. 1997. *The Magic of the State*. New York: Routledge.

———. 2005. *Law in a Lawless Land: Diary of a Limpieza in Colombia*. Chicago: University of Chicago Press.

Tawil-Souri, Helga. 2017. Checkpoint Time. *Qui Parle* 26(2): 383–422. doi:10.1215/10418385-4208442

Tilly, Charles. 1985. "War Making and State Making as Organized Crime." In *Bringing the State Back In*, edited by Peter B. Evans, Dietrich Rueschemeyer, and Theda Skocpol, 169–91. Cambridge: Cambridge University Press.

Trigg, Dylan. 2012. *The Memory of Place: A Phenomenology of the Uncanny*. Athens: Ohio University Press.

Varisco, Daniel Martin. 2005. *Islam Obscured: The Rhetoric of Anthropological Representation*. New York: Palgrave.

Voell, Stéphane, and Iwona Kaliszewska, eds. 2015. *State and Legal Practice in the Caucasus: Anthropological Perspectives on Law and Politics*. Farnham, UK: Ashgate.

Ware, Robert Bruce, and Enver Kisriev. 2001. "Ethnic Parity and Democratic Pluralism in Dagestan: A Consociational Approach." *Europe-Asia Studies* 53(1): 105–31.

———. 2009. *Dagestan: Russian Hegemony and Islamic Resistance in the North Caucasus*. New York: M. E. Sharpe.

Weissberg-Cybulski, Andrzej. 1952. *Conspiracy of Silence*. Translated by Edward Fitzgerald. London: Hamish Hamilton.

Yarlykapov, Akhmet A. 2000. *Problema vakhkhabizma na severnom kavkaze*. Moscow: Institut etnologii i antropologii, RAN.

———. 2008. *Islam u stepnykh nogaytsev*. Moscow: Institut etnologii i antropologii, RAN.

Yemelianova, Galina. 2002. *Russia and Islam: A Historical Survey*. London: Palgrave.

Yurchak, Alexei. 2006. *Everything Was Forever, until It Was No More: The Last Soviet Generation*. Princeton, NJ: Princeton University Press.

Zalimkhanov, Zaur, and Kaflan Khanbabayev. 2000. *Politizatsiya islama na Severnom Kavkaze*. Makhachkala, Dagestan: Dagestanskiy gosudarstvennyy pedagogicheskiy universitet.

Zapaśnik, Stanisław. 2014. *"Walczący islam" w Azji Centralnej: Problem społecznej genezy zjawiska*. Wrocław, Poland: Monografie FNP.

Zelkina, Anna. 2000. *In Quest for God and Freedom: The Sufi Response to the Russian Advance in the North Caucasus*. London: Hurst.

Žižek, Slavoj. 1997. *The Plague of Fantasies*. London: Verso.

Index

adats, 55, 98, 109
adhan. *See* prayer
alcohol, 6, 22, 58, 70–71, 75, 85, 90, 101, 110, 112–113, 119–121, 123–124, 128, 131
alms. *See* zakat
assassination, 21, 123

Basayev, Shamil, 83, 87
Benjamin, Walter, 84
bloodletting. *See hijama*.
bombings. *See* explosions
brainwashing, vii, 70, 73–74

censorship, 97
Chechnya: wars, 25, 53; Salafist allegiance to, 64; under Ramzan Kadyrov, 101, 123
checkpoints, 30, 44–48, 51, 126, 129
Christianity, 39–40, 55, 92, 119
communities. *See jamaats*
corruption, ix, 16–17, 20–21, 23, 25, 28, 30, 35, 47, 73–74, 86, 96, 101, 105–108, 114, 116, 120, 122–123, 126–127, 131–132
counterterrorism, x, 9, 16–18, 21–23, 29, 32–36, 38, 42 44–45, 47, 49–50, 73, 80–81, 126, 135
criminal code, 103, 107, 114
cross-dressing, 124

Dagestan: history of state building, 24; international interest in, 51; Arab invasions of, 54–55; Russian conquest of, 55–56; Islamist invasion, 63
dhikr. *See* prayer
divination. *See* fortune-tellers
drugs, 119

economy, 25, 28, 86; economic development, 26; informal, 28
elections, 25
emigration. *See* migration

employment and unemployment, 6, 23–24, 26, 38, 72–73, 109–110, 114–115, 117, 122, 134
espionage, 16, 31
ethnicity, 4, 55, 59–62, 67, 93, 98, 117; ethnic conflict, 61; *See also* USSR: ethnic policy of
exorcism, ix–x, 6, 39–43, 95, 103
explosions, 8–10, 21, 33, 43, 45, 48, 123
extortion, 22, 73–74, 75, 90, 94–95, 101. *See also* organized crime

fasting, 80, 88, 110
fieldwork, 11–19, 31–32, 34, 77–78, 95; ethical dilemmas, 14–16
firearms. *See* weapons
fortune-tellers, 94–95, 119, 131
FSB (Federal Security Bureau). *See* law enforcement

gambling, 75, 101
gender roles. *See* social roles
guerrillas. *See* militants
gunfire, 8–9, 33, 43–44, 47, 126

hadith, 88
hajj, 57–58, 85, 88
health care system, ix, 106–108
hegemony, 42
hijab, vii, xi, 15, 35, 39, 75, 78, 82, 91, 101, 105, 112, 131
hijama, 6, 15, 103, 105–106
hospitality, 15, 30, 32

ijma, 88
images, defacement of, 6, 90
Imam Shamil, 55–56, 117
imams, 6, 55, 64, 80, 85, 110, 112–113, 119–122, 124–125
imprisonment, 22, 51, 117
infrastructure, 20, 24, 110, 121–122, 127
insurgency, 22–22, 26, 29, 33, 50, 64

interrogation, 30, 32, 35
ISIS, 1, 21, 22, 134–135
Islam: role in everyday life, 53–54, 56, 58, 66, 68, 75, 82, 85, 89; history in Dagestan, 54–56; persecution of, 41, 55–56, 63–64, 83; "traditional Islam," 62, 68–69, 76, 78, 83; conversion to, 15, 78–79, 82, 91–92, 96, 115, 134; essentialization by Western scholars, 87–88
Islamic banking, 93
Islamic education, 20, 24, 55, 57, 64, 67, 75, 93, 96
Islamic holidays, 75, 80, 85, 110, 112
Islamic law. *See* sharia
Islamic media, 57–58, 64, 75, 77–79, 81–82, 103, 120
Islamic medicine, 39, 78–79, 81, 85, 91, 106
Islamic political parties and organizations, 57–58, 83
Islamic rituals, 58, 62, 70, 80, 88, 117
Islamic state, 65, 85–86, 91, 93, 107–108, 131
Islamic stores, 15, 22, 77–79, 81–82, 103
Islamic "revivals," 53–54, 56–58, 68, 75
Islamization, 19, 54–55
ijtihad, 88

jamaats, 7, 24–25, 56, 61–62, 108, 112, 113, 119, 122, 130; history of, 108–110, 117, 127
jihad, 22, 55, 90, 94, 135
jinns, ix–x, 39–42, 98, 106

Kabardino-Balkaria, 83
Kadyrov, Ramzan. *See* Chechnya: under Ramzan Kadyrov
khilaf, 88
kidnapping, 2, 22, 34, 51, 65, 123
kolkhoz, 109
Koran, ix–x, 42, 55, 58, 70, 79–80, 85, 88, 92–93, 103–104, 106, 114, 125; translation of, 98

land ownership, 109, 113
language, viii, 59, 117, 126; Russian, 24, 40–41, 62, 78
law enforcement, 2, 9, 15, 17–18, 21–23, 25, 29–32, 41, 47–49, 51, 73, 78, 80, 93, 98, 101, 105, 108, 113, 122–123, 126–127, 133–134
letter writing, 51
lezginka, 124
living arrangements, viii, xi, 9

madhhabs, 67, 89
madrassas. *See* Islamic education
magic, 11, 39
marshrutkas, 5–6, 9–10, 15, 34, 43, 48, 75, 79, 105
maslihat, 116
matchmaking, 6
mawlid, vii, 69, 124–125
media, state-controlled, 50
migration, 6, 25–26, 28, 51, 64, 109–110, 112, 122, 127
militants, viii, 8, 21–22, 35–37, 50, 64–65, 80, 83, 93–94, 101, 116; support for, 33, 65, 101
miswak stick, x, 39, 78–79, 104
modernization, 99–100, 121, 125
mosques, 5, 41, 55–57, 62, 64, 67, 75, 81–82, 109–110
motherhood, 11
murder, 18, 22, 30, 34–35, 94, 114, 116, 123
murids, 67, 77
music, 124
MVD (Ministry of Internal Affairs), 29, 31

namaz. *See* prayer
nasheeds, 71, 75, 77, 79
national movements, 24, 53, 58–62, 68
natural medicine, 6, 107
nepotism, 23, 107
"new Muslims," 65, 67–68, 76, 82–83, 85, 115, 131

organized crime, 20–22, 25, 75, 116; *See also* extortion

periphery, 26
photography, 31–32
pilgrimage. *See* hajj
pollution, 101
polygamy, 6, 14, 75, 106, 114, 121
poniatiya. *See* criminal code
poverty, 86
prayer, viii, 13, 39, 41, 52, 58, 75, 77, 79–80, 85, 88, 91, 96, 109–110, 115, 117, 123
pre-Islamic practices, 55, 67, 117, 119, 125
press, 17
proscriptions: cultural, 10, 44, 95; religious, 42, 91, 101–102, 104–105, 124
prosecutorial misconduct, 37
prostitution, 75, 101
public debate, 16–17
Putin, Vladimir, 25, 36, 49–53

INDEX

racketeering. *See* extortion
rape, 116–117
reconciliation. *See maslihat*
religious practices, non-Muslim, 103
remittances, 28
renaming of streets, 5
resistance, 42
ROVD (Regional Department of Internal Affairs), 32, 35, 37
Russians, 15, 41, 78, 93, 101, 121

Salafism, vii, 18–19, 30–31, 41, 56, 62–74, 76–81, 89, 92, 94, 110, 120, 123; external attributes of, 69–70, 80, 92, 104–105; use of "Wahhabi" as an epithet, 70, 74, 104; Sufi-Wahhabi dichotomy, 63, 68–70, 76–77, 80–83, 95
salah. See prayer
schools, 109–110, 120
secularism, 5, 24, 41, 79, 82, 85–86, 112, 120, 134
security, 86, 94, 101
shahada, 88
sharia, 3, 20, 24, 54–55, 63, 66, 85–89, 129–133; opposition to, 90–91; as a state-level project, 90–101; as a personal project, 103–107; as a community-level project, 108–128
shaykhs, 57, 64, 66–67, 76, 78, 80, 116
shirk, 67, 92
siloviki. See law enforcement
social justice and injustice, 86, 97, 105
social roles, 11, 14, 105
socialism, 93, 100, 131
society, reform of, 99–100
special operations. *See* counterterrorism
Spiritual Board of the Muslims of Dagestan (DUMD), 57, 62–64, 69–70, 72–75, 77, 80, 82, 98
state: experience of, 20, 22–23, 24, 26, 29, 38, 50–52, 86, 100, 105, 130; disintegration of, 24–25; legitimacy of, 29; idea of, 30, 131; distrust of, 34, 36, 48, 65, 74, 85; longing for a strong state, 51; ineffectiveness of, 101, 122–123, 130; autonomy from, 110, 113–115, 127–128, 131–132
Sufism, 40–42, 55–56, 62–64, 66–70, 76, 78–80; *See also* Salafism: Sufi-Wahhabi dichotomy
sunnah. See prayer

talismans, 98
Tariqatists, 67–68, 81, 82, 89
taxation, 23, 25
terrorism, 2–3, 63; false accusations, 36; watch list, x–xi
tobacco, 70, 75, 110, 112, 119
torture, 30, 34–37, 51–52, 65, 83, 129–130; history of, 37–38
tukhums, 28, 59, 70, 109, 112, 119, 125, 135

unemployment. *See* employment
USSR: collapse of, 24, 53–54, 56, 68, 99; memory of, 52, 86, 89, 96, 99, 121–122, 128; ethnic policy of, 59–61
usury, 93

veshalki, 37
violence, 3, 9–10, 17–18, 20, 23, 29–30, 33–34, 37, 47–49, 81, 86, 99, 107, 128–129; perpetrated by the state, 38, 42–45, 50–51, 83–85, 130; internalization of, 29, 38, 43–44, 48, 51; visual traces of, 45, 73, 129; anticipation of, 47–48, 51; domestic, 119

Wahhabism. *See* Salafism
war on terror. *See* counterterrorism
weapons, 8–9, 31–32, 35
weddings, 71, 123–124. *See also* Islamic rituals

yedinobozhniki, 39–40, 42

zakat, 20, 22, 88

www.ingramcontent.com/pod-product-compliance
Lightning Source LLC
Chambersburg PA
CBHW040314170426
43195CB00021B/2973